# Union and Open-Shop Construction

WITHDRAWN

# Union and Open-Shop Construction

## Compensation, Work Practices, and Labor Markets

**Clinton C. Bourdon**
Harvard University

**Raymond E. Levitt**
Massachusetts Institute of
Technology

**LexingtonBooks**
D.C. Heath and Company
Lexington, Massachusetts
Toronto

**Library of Congress Cataloging in Publication Data**

Bourdon, Clinton C
    Union and open-shop construction.

    Bibliography: p.
    Includes index.
    1. Wages—Construction workers—United States. 2. Open and closed
shop—United States. 3. Restrictive practices in industrial relations—United
States. 4. Labor costs—United States. 5. Trade-unions—Construction
workers—United States. 6. Construction industry—United States. I. Levitt,
Raymond E., joint author. II. Title.
HD4966.B892U54      331.2'042'40973      79-1724
ISBN 0-669-02918-1

Published simultaneously in Canada.

Printed in the United States of America.

International Standard Book Number: 0-669-02918-1

Library of Congress Catalog Card Number: 79-1724

# Contents

# List of Figures and Tables

# Preface and Acknowledgments

This book is based, in part, on a contract research study undertaken for the U.S. Department of Housing and Urban Development under the direction of the authors at the Department of Civil Engineering of the Massachusetts Institute of Technology. Full acknowledgment of all the contributors to and collaborators in that project is contained in the research report, "A Comparison of Wages and Labor Management Practices in Union and Nonunion Construction" (HUD Contract #H-2327-R, MIT Department of Civil Engineering, June 1, 1978).

This book was prepared with the assistance of a small research grant from the Harvard-MIT Joint Center for Urban Studies. Clint Bourdon is the author of chapters 1 through 4; Ray Levitt collaborated on chapters 5 through 7. All errors and interpretations are the sole responsibility of the authors.

# 1 Introduction

During the last few years, the economic competition and political conflict between the open-shop and union sectors of the construction industry have attracted considerable public attention. Many local communities have seen disruptions caused by picketing of open-shop job-sites. Nationally, struggles in Congress over passage of situs-picketing legislation and repeal of the Davis-Bacon Act, coupled with the defeat of labor law reform, have focused attention not only on labor relations and building costs in construction but also on their interaction. Construction also appears to represent yet another industry where erstwhile union dominance has been eroded by the forces of competition represented by the entry of nonunion firms. And, in a political climate where public policy is encouraged to fight inflation by promoting competition, there is no dearth of voices to celebrate the rise of the open shop.

Yet, despite the apparent growth of nonunion activity in all branches of the construction industry, there is very little comparative analysis of exactly how—or even whether—open-shop and union firms differ significantly in operation and efficiency. Recent academic studies, such as Mills's *Industrial Relations and Manpower in Construction* and Northrup and Foster's *Open Shop Construction*, deal primarily with one sector to the exclusion of the other. Current journalistic accounts, such as those published periodically in *Fortune* or *Business Week*, while factual, tend to be selective in their attention to union abuses or violence. Ironically, past academic research, such as that by Haber and Levinson in *Labor Relations and Productivity in the Building Trades*, does not substantiate the importance of union restrictive work practices that conventional wisdom would suggest.

This volume attempts, in the context of a broad overview of the construction industry, to compare and contrast current union and open-shop wages and work practices. Based on sample data from both a wage questionnaire and from interviews with over two hundred construction firms in eight metropolitan areas,[1] it portrays union and nonunion differences and similarities in compensation, work rules, hiring, training, technology; and total labor costs in relation to particular product markets in construction (residential, commercial-industrial, or heavy and highway) and with specific attention to the relative size and resources of construction firms.

While all construction firms face common tasks in the management of a construction workforce, their labor policies can differ significantly by type and

1

scale of construction work. For example, a small firm engaged in residential rehabilitation may find a particular union work rule or wage level restrictive or costly; a large contractor working on a multi-story commercial building may not. For this reason, in making comparisons between union and non-union construction firms it is crucial to delineate the specific context in which the comparisons are made. The construction "industry" in the U.S. is actually a very complex ecology of submarkets. Each of these have different levels and elasticities of product demand; different technologies of production with varying mixes of worker skill, materials, and equipment; and different size distributions and competitive climates for firms. Understanding the contrasting characteristics of union and nonunion contractors requires more than the simple reporting of either sample observations or labor relations preferences. Analysis of both of these must be grounded in the technology and productive structure of the industry.

To provide a context for the union open-shop comparisons, chapter 2 depicts the extent of open-shop growth in different geographic areas, by types of construction, and by firm size. Differences in union and nonunion wages and benefits are described and analyzed in chapter 3, with attention to important distinctions in skill levels and occupational structure. Chapter 4 reviews findings on work practices and labor market structure, contrasting the casual union labor market with its relatively high interfirm mobility of workers to the open-shop alternative of firm-specific occupations and internal job progression. Examples of comparative labor costs are given in chapter 5 as an indication of the range of elements which should comprise union and nonunion cost comparisons. The implications of the survey findings for an analysis of the impact of the Davis-Bacon Act are presented in chapter 6, while the last chapter provides some examples of recent institutional responses to open-shop growth in the construction industry. Appendixes A, B, and C contain the wage data and the contractor interview schedule as well as a brief description of survey methodology.

## Craft Labor Markets

As a theme throughout the book, a comparison is drawn between the labor market activities and impact of the building-trades craft unions, and the open shop alternative. The implicit argument in this comparison is that, ideally, craft unions can work through various market institutions, such as jurisdictional rules, uniform hourly wage rates, and the hiring hall, to increase the efficiency of a casual labor market for skilled workers. In other words, if a market is characterized by both a high degree of instability in employment and heterogeneity of products, certain common rules and institutions may, by reducing the need for continual adjustments to a diversity of tasks or external conditions, actually enhance productive efficiency.[2] Thus, a uniform hourly wage rate, such as that set for journeymen in construction collective-bargaining contracts, can economize on individual worker and employer bargaining and search, if all the workers who earn the wage are homogeneous, that is, have equivalent skills and motivation.[3] It is, of course, the function of formal apprenticeship training in construction to provide those common and equivalent skills. And the purpose of trade jurisdictions is to protect enough property rights over specific skills and jobs so as to encourage considerable investment in apprentice training, even though the worker may not have the security of a relatively permanent attachment to a specific firm.

This ideal portrayal of craft labor markets and their potential for high efficieny fails to fit reality in several ways, of course.[4] It serves primarily to call attention to the importance of the role that institutions such as apprenticeship or jurisdictions can play in construction. These structures need not be seen as simply attempts by building trades unions to raise wages by restricting the supply of labor. Though they can be used for that purpose by unions—or in the absence of unions, by employers for opposite purposes—these institutions also have a basic functional role. Nonetheless, their operation can become so degraded in practice that their impact may have negative effects on the efficiency of union labor markets and the productivity of union workers. For example, if a uniform union wage is considerably out of line with average worker productivity, or if the skills of union journeymen vary substantially and this cannot be reflected in the hourly wage, then any union contribution to efficiency will be reduced, if not eliminated. In these cases, the union sector will be ripe for competition from open-shop firms.

How nonunion firms enter and operate in a largely union industry like construction has never been fully explored. Clearly, they can attempt to compete only at the margins of the industry or in isolated subsectors by simply paying lower wages and by resisting union organizing attempts if any occur. But if they grow to compete with many union firms across a wide range of construction activity, open-shop contractors may have to create labor policies and institutions which are similar to those in union firms. As an analogy, some large nonunion employers in manufacturing now have grievance procedures, job-posting and bidding systems, and even employee-representation committees largely because these are effective means of managing large groups of workers. Open-shop construction firms may also respond by adopting work-force practices which virtually duplicate union institutions. Conversely, they may innovate and develop new or different policies for hiring, training, and compensation which best fit their type and scale of construction. These new nonunion practices and institutions may result in equivalent or greater efficiency than in the union sector. The survey results reported in the following chapters explore these potential union and open-shop differences and similarities, and advance tentative conclusions on their impact on production and costs.


**What Is "Union"?**

Finally, before discussing the trends in construction activity over the last decade which bear on the growth of the open shop, it is important to note one crucial issue of definition or terminology. Throughout this book the words "union" and "nonunion" (or "open-shop") are used to designate firms which are or are not, respectively, signatory to a full collective bargaining agreement with one or more building trades unions. While this distinction may appear obvious, the complexity of the construction industry can make these arbitrary divisions nonsensical. Union members may work for nonunion firms; nonunion firms may sign temporary or partial agreements with union locals or internationals. Nonunion or union subcontractors will work with union or open-shop general contractors, while nonunion workers may work, usually temporarily, on union job-sites. Even one firm may operate "double-breasted" and have, under suitable legal and functional arrangements, union and open-shop divisions. As Mills (1977) notes,

> such issues of [union] definition and classification are best left to philosophers and to those statisticians and econometricians who insist on dividing the world into union and nonunion categories in order to compile data series. What is important in construction itself is the development of methods of doing business which do not rigidify the union-nonunion distinction, but instead blur it in order to make it of less practical significance.[5]

Despite this flexiblity in mixing union and nonunion workers and firms, or in changing union contract terms, the use of these categories throughout the following pages will carry a clear distinction: firms designated as union are those which were signatory to a collective bargaining agreement; nonunion or open-shop firms are not. All other data or findings which may confuse this distinction will be noted.


**Cyclical Fluctuations in Construction Volume**

Often overlooked in making static comparisons of the relative share of union and open-shop activity in any industry are the general trends in dollar volume and employment which provide the dynamic context during which major changes in shares can take place. Recognizing such trends is particularly important in construction because of the impact that changes in building volume and geographic location have on the entry of firms in the industry, the employment opportunities of workers, and the relative power of unions.

Over the last decade, the construction industry has been through cylical fluctuations unprecedented in the post-World War II period (see figure 1-1). The rapid rise in nonresidential building volume in the mid-1960s was accompanied by a sustained expansion in public construction and a cyclical peak in residential construction. Unemployment levels in construction dropped below 4 percent, an unusually low level, for four consecutive years (see table 1-1). Then, in the mid-1970s, after the residential sector had experienced a brief but massive peak in building activity, all sectors of the industry declined precipitously. Between 1973 and 1976, nonresidential construction—all of the major commercial, industrial, and heavy work—fell by over 30 percent while public construction declined steadily from 1968 on. Construction unemployment rates nationally rose to as much as 18 percent in the depths of the recession in 1975 and were substantially higher in major urban areas.

This rapid boom and bust cycle had three effects on relative union strength in the industry. First, the sustained increase in building volume in the late 1960s in all sectors provided an ample market opportunity for the entry and growth of new firms both in residential building, where firm size is small and entry is easy, and in public construction where open bidding lists provide a very accessible competitive opportunity to new firms. Second, the strong increase in dollar volume and the low construction unemployment in the late sixties touched off a period of high wage increases and lengthy strikes in the union sector of the industry. These wage gains would come back to haunt the union sector when, third, the recession drastically reduced the volume of that very commercial and industrial building which had triggered those collective bargaining settlements. Coupled with the decline of public construction, union mechanics were becoming unemployed in large numbers. Many responded, not by voting to reduce union wage scales, but by working on their own account or for nonunion firms at lower wages. Thus, the open shop was provided with an additional source of skilled labor exactly at a time when it had grown to a point of being competitive for the reduced volume of residential and commercial building which did continue through the middle and late 1970s. In sum, both extremes in construction volume between 1968 and 1978 worked to the advantage of open-shop competition.

Increases in union hourly rates in the late 1960s, driven by the high volume of construction demand, were a major cause of subsequent open-shop growth. But equally or more important in understanding the character

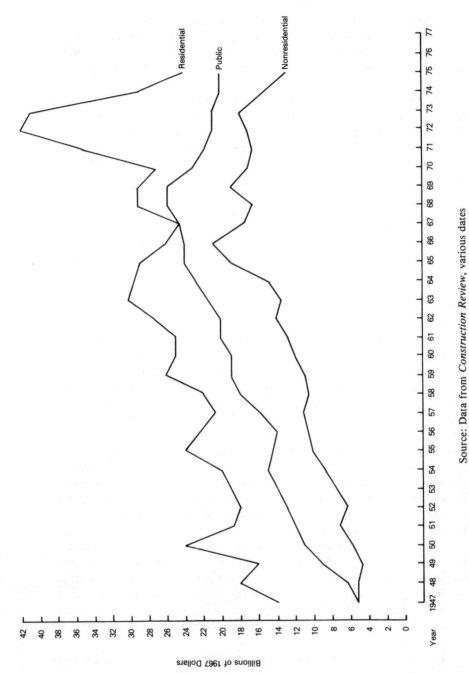

Source: Data from *Construction Review*, various dates

**Figure 1-1.** Residential, Nonresidential, and Public Value Put in Place: 1947-1975

**Table 1-1**
**Annual Rates of Unemployment and of Union Hourly Wage Increases, Contract Construction, 1950 to 1979**

| Year | Percent Wage Increase | Unemployment Rate |
|------|-----------------------|-------------------|
| 1950 | 4.2 | 12.2 |
| 1951 | 6.6 | 7.2 |
| 1952 | 6.2 | 6.7 |
| 1953 | 5.1 | 7.2 |
| 1954 | 3.8 | 12.9 |
| 1955 | 3.5 | 10.9 |
| 1956 | 4.7 | 10.0 |
| 1957 | -5.1 | 10.9 |
| 1958 | 4.6 | 15.3 |
| 1959 | 4.9 | 13.4 |
| 1960 | 4.1 | 13.5 |
| 1961 | 4.0 | 15.7 |
| 1962 | 3.7 | 13.5 |
| 1963 | 3.6 | 13.3 |
| 1964 | 3.7 | 11.2 |
| 1965 | 3.1 | 10.1 |
| 1966 | 5.2 | 8.0 |
| 1967 | 5.6 | 7.4 |
| 1968 | 6.6 | 6.9 |
| 1969 | 7.6 | 6.0 |
| 1970 | 11.6 | 9.7 |
| 1971 | 11.8 | 10.4 |
| 1972 | 6.4 | 10.3 |
| 1973 | 5.0 | 8.8 |
| 1974 | 7.8 | 10.6 |
| 1975 | 8.6 | 18.1 |
| 1976 | 6.5 | 14.4 |
| 1977 | n.a. | 12.7 |
| 1978 | n.a. | 10.6 |
| 1979 | n.a. | 10.1[a] |

Source: U.S. Bureau of Labor Statistics, *Handbook of Labor Statistics, 1977*, Washington, D.C., 1977; *Monthly Labor Review*, October 1979, p. 86; and BLS, *Union Wages and Hours: Building Trades*, Washington, D.C., 1978.

[a]Preliminary figures, January through August only.

of open-shop entry in the industry is not the average rate of wage increase but the rigidity of the union wage structure. Construction wages tend to move up together. If a few trades face market conditions which permit them to gain large increases, these increments may be duplicated—sometimes to the penny—by other local unions in the area. As a result, wage levels or increases which may be justified by change in skills or demand for a particular trade in a particular locality tend to spread across all unions in the industry. During the 1960s, for example, average union hourly wage rates for skilled building trades journeymen nearly doubled, but the rates for laborers also doubled. Throughout the seventies, increases in laborers' rates continued to keep pace with those of journeymen. Thus, by the end of the 1970s, many relatively unskilled building laborers were earning nearly ten or more dollars per hour. Similarly, throughout this period the average wage increases for plumbers and for pipefitters were virtually identical (both are, after all, members of the same international union, although they usually comprise separate union locals at the local level). Yet pipefitters and plumbers have faced considerably different trends in demand for their work, along with quite varied changes in skills and technology. Pipefitters have been helped by increases in dollar volume and in skills demanded because of the expansion in complex chemical facilities and power plants; while commercial plumbers have met severe competition from the use of materials like prefabricated metal and plastic piping, which are low cost substitutes for plumber fabricating skills. Maintaining a wage structure between and within unions which (while by no means entirely rigid) provides for relatively uniform rates of increase, creates ample opportunity for lower wage competition. In construction especially, firms may move eventually to subcontract even small parts of projects where a union has priced itself out of that particular market.

**Secular Trends in Geographic Location**

Over the same time period as these major fluctuations, substantial shifts were occurring in the location of construction activity. Between 1968 and 1978, for example, the relative volume of nonresidential building in the Northeast and North Central sections of the United States increased little, if at all. But during this period, as table 1-2 shows, commercial and industrial construction nearly tripled in the South and quadrupled in the West. In par-

**Table 1-2**
**Volume Put in Place, Nonresidential Building by Region, 1960-1978**
*(billions of current dollars)*

| Year | Northeast | North Central | South | West |
|------|-----------|---------------|-------|------|
| 1960 | 0.215 | 1.415 | 1.474 | 1.368 |
| 1962 | 0.222 | 1.406 | 1.553 | 1.595 |
| 1964 | 1.345 | 1.846 | 1.884 | 1.752 |
| 1966 | 1.912 | 2.399 | 2.311 | 2.052 |
| 1968 | 2.466 | 2.697 | 3.067 | 2.150 |
| 1970 | 2.540 | 2.486 | 3.424 | 2.578 |
| 1972 | 2.251 | 3.350 | 5.069 | 3.290 |
| 1974 | 2.903 | 4.078 | 5.597 | 3.801 |
| 1976 | 1.941 | 3.890 | 4.817 | 4.317 |
| 1978 | 2.774 | 5.511 | 8.296 | 7.417 |

Source: *Construction Review*, various dates.

ticular, the rapid growth of large-scale industrial and petrochemical construction in the South, particularly in the Gulf Coast area, provided a major market for open-shop firms.

Another long-run change in construction location which is harder to document, but is no less important, is the continuing suburbanization of U.S. commercial and office activity. The spread of low-rise construction along highway strip development or in shopping centers provided a new construction market for smaller firms, with limited engineering or technical resources, far from union-dominated center-city areas.

Of these three elements of the dynamic context in which open-shop growth has taken place, only one—suburbanization—is not likely to continue in its past form or rate. Thus, further growth of nonresidential construction in the South coupled with recurring and abrupt fluctuations in economic activity will continue to present opportunities for open-shop expansion and to pose challenges for union adjustment and reaction.

**Notes**

1. The metropolitan areas surveyed in the fall and summer of 1976 were: Atlanta, Baltimore, Boston, Denver, Grand Rapids, Kansas City (Mo.), New Orleans, Portland (Oreg.). The survey sampled only firms located within the boundaries of these areas as defined by each Standard Metropolitan Statistical Area (SMSA).

2. See Williamson et al. in "Understanding the Employment Relation: The Analysis of Idiosyncratic Exchange," for a detailed description of the contribution of institutional structures to labor market performance; also, Stinchcombe, in "Bureaucratic and Craft Means of Production," explores the role of broadly trained, self-supervising craft workers as substitutes for detailed bureaucratic controls. The development of these ideas into a theory of management control, which relates methods of management control to the type of production process, has been developed by Ouchi in "The Relations between Organizational Structure and Organizational Control."

3. Hall describes this alternative to markets with flexible prices in "The Role of Prevailing Prices and Wages in the Efficient Organization of Markets."

4. One of the most important differences is that the building trade unions themselves are hardly "pure" craft unions. Many of the unions, formally or informally, incorporate narrowly defined occupations, such as floorlayers or crane operators, as well as more broadly trained journeymen in carpentry, pipefitting, or other trades.

5. D.Q. Mills, "Collective Bargaining in Construction," in G. Somers, ed. *Contemporary Collective Bargaining*, 1977.

# 2

# Industrial Organization of the Construction Industry

In terms of type and size of products, the construction industry is extremely diverse; output ranges from small residential building alterations to the construction of nuclear power plants. The diversity of the industry implies substantial differences in the structure and behavior of construction firms. In turn, differences between products and firms may affect occupational structure, skills demanded (and hence wages) and labor market institutions for workers in the industry. Thus, some understanding of the market structure of the construction industry is necessary both to interpret the context in which union and open-shop competition can take place and to accurately characterize the type of open-shop growth which has occurred.

## Product Market Distribution and Firm Size

Perhaps the most characteristic aspect of the construction industry is the prevalence of small firms. Of the 920,806 contractors in the United States in 1972, 82 percent had less than four employees and 97 percent reported less than one million dollars in annual receipts.[1] Yet this multitude of firms of miniscule size should not disguise the fact that total employment and dollar volume in the industry are actually relatively concentrated. While companies which reported more than fifty employees made up only .02 percent of the total number of firms, they employed nearly half the labor force. Of the $164 billion in total receipts in 1972, over 50 percent was generated by 3 percent of the largest firms.

This extreme discrepancy between the vast number of construction firms and the relatively small number which dominate the volume in the industry prevents any facile conclusion about the competitive environment in construction as a whole. Moreover, though construction is usually characterized as a local market, many relatively small firms regularly move over state and regional areas to bid on work within their specialty. While this strengthens competitive tendencies in particular areas, it also tends to channel that competition within barriers defined by product type. Thus it is not unusual in the industry to have only a few firms bidding on specific projects, especially if these are unusual or specialized types of construction projects for clients with strong preferences in regard to final cost, quality, completion time, or union status. As a consequence, in an industry which on its face may appear to be extremely competitive, there are in fact innumerable niches for area or product specialization. And while entry to many parts of the industry is relatively easy, particularly in small-scale general and subcontracting, due to the low fixed-capital requirements of the business, expansion is time-consuming and risky. A firm's dollar volume of work usually grows slowly, since its ability to bid successfully on larger or more complex projects depends not only on its current prices or cost estimates but also on the perception of others that it has completed smaller projects well. Thus, some parts of the industry may respond only very slowly to competitive trends which may have already run their course in other subsectors of construction. For this reason, when describing the open-shop sector in construction it is important to be quite specific as to geographic location, type of building activity, and size of firm. The very heterogeneity of the industry and the large degree of product differentiation within it provide numerous and quite varied contexts for open-shop entry and competition with union firms. The following sections chronicle the type of open-shop growth which has occurred in particular subsectors of the industry and provide estimates of the proportion of construction employment which is currently nonunion.

## Growth and Evolution of the Open Shop

An excellent example of the growth of open-shop construction is the current domination of much of the residential housing market by nonunion construction firms. With the exception of some large midwestern cities and much of the West Coast, the construction of single-family housing and garden and low-rise apartments is now the province of open-shop contractors. Yet a little over twenty-five years ago, home building in most Eastern and North Central states was substantially union. For the early 1950s, Haber and Levinson report that 50 to 75 percent of home building in Boston, for example, and 95 to 100 percent in Cleveland was estimated to have been undertaken by union contractors.[2] Unfortunately, there are no valid time series which portray the evolution of this trend over the intervening years. Yet the data from the 1976 survey confirm that union activity in homebuilding and other residential construction is now very low—only 10 percent of the union firms in the sample reported more than 60 percent of their volume from this work—and is largely confined to the western cities in the sample: Kansas City, Denver, and Portland (see table 2-1). These three cities account for 83 percent of the union firms reporting a concentration in residential work. In contrast, nearly 50 percent of the total open-shop firms in the eight areas were classified as working mainly in residential construction; moreover, these firms were found in substantial numbers in almost all of the areas surveyed.

By 1976, however, open-shop activity also had expanded to encompass large amounts of commercial and industrial building. This was a type of construction also acknowledged to be substantially union up until the late 1960s in all of the eight metropolitan areas surveyed. But in 1976, there were considerable numbers of nonunion general and subcontractors in commercial building: of more than fifteen hundred predominantly commercial building firms surveyed, 40 percent were open shop (see table 2-2). These open-shop firms were found in most of the eight areas, and particularly in those areas where there was a large amount of nonunion residential construction.

This spread of the nonunion sector over a wider range of construction product markets, from residential to commercial building, is illustrated by the relatively less specialization by type of construction among some open-shop firms. For example, in Boston in 1976, 70 percent of the union general contractors and 87 percent of the union subcontractors surveyed reported that they did more than 60 percent of their work in commercial and industrial building only. For the open-shop contractors, only 39 and 56 percent, respectively, were so specialized. This difference may reflect a step in the evolution of many open-shop firms from their start and growth in residential construction to their current ability to compete with union companies in commercial building work.

Coincident with the evident spread of open-shop work from residential to commercial and industrial building was an equivalent broadening of the geographic locus of nonunion activity. Although the survey of firms was confined to those within eight metropolitan areas, interviews with contractors and officers of local associations produced qualitative evidence that open-shop growth was particularly strong in suburban and rural areas. Even in states as disparate in history and character as Georgia and Massachusetts, many union contractors told the same story of no longer being able to compete outside the center city area of Boston or Atlanta. Until a decade or so ago, they said, both their suburban fringe and all of the smaller cities, such as Macon and Savannah or Worcester and Lowell, were solidly union. Yet, in 1976, central city high-rise construction in those states—as well as in the others surveyed—remained substantially union even when the rest of the state or region was predominantly open-shop.

**Relative Firm Size**

Despite this apparent evolution in both the location and nature of open-shop activity, in 1976 most nonunion firms in the sample were considerably smaller than union construction firms (see table 2-3). For example, in Baltimore, the median size of open-shop firms doing predominantly commercial and industrial work was fifteen field employees with a 1975 median

**Table 2-1**
**Union Firms: Distribution by Dollar Volume and Product Market, Eight Standard Metropolitan Statistical Areas, 1976**
*(number of firms)*

| Product Market | Dollar Volume | | | | | Proportion by Product Market (percent) |
|---|---|---|---|---|---|---|
| | *less than $100,000* | *$100,000-$500,000* | *$500,000-$1 million* | *$1 million-$5 million* | *more than $5 million* | |
| *Residential* | | | | | | 10 |
| General | 2 | 13 | 7 | 12 | 3 | |
| Subcontractors | 14 | 42 | 11 | 13 | 1 | |
| *Heavy and Highway* | | | | | | 9 |
| General | 1 | 12 | 12 | 28 | 30 | |
| Subcontractors | 1 | 6 | 5 | 11 | 3 | |
| *Commercial-Industrial* | | | | | | 20 |
| General | 7 | 20 | 41 | 84 | 72 | |
| Subcontractors | 29 | 197 | 163 | 246 | 62 | |
| Proportion by Size (percent) | 4 | 25 | 21 | 35 | 15 | 100 |

Source: 1976 survey by the Department of Housing and Urban Development and the Massachusetts Institute of Technology.

**Table 2-2**
**Nonunion Firms: Distribution by Dollar Volume and Product Market, Eight Standard Metropolitan Statistical Areas, 1976**
*(number of firms)*

| Product Market | Dollar Volume | | | | | Proportion by Product Market (percent) |
|---|---|---|---|---|---|---|
| | less than $100,000 | $100,000-$500,000 | $500,000-$1 million | $1 million-$5 million | more than $5 million | |
| *Residential* | | | | | | 47 |
| General | 98 | 128 | 59 | 57 | 14 | |
| Subcontractors | 14 | 42 | 11 | 13 | 1 | |
| *Heavy and Highway* | | | | | | 5 |
| General | 0 | 11 | 9 | 21 | 2 | |
| Subcontractors | 1 | 8 | 4 | 1 | 0 | |
| *Commercial-Industrial* | | | | | | 48 |
| General | 18 | 102 | 70 | 74 | 19 | |
| Subcontractors | 49 | 168 | 67 | 45 | 1 | |
| Proportion by Size (percent) | 19 | 42 | 19 | 17 | 3 | 100 |

Source: 1976 survey by the Department of Housing and Urban Development and the Massachusetts Institute of Technology.

**Table 2-3**
**Median Size of Respondent Firms, 1976 Survey**

| Survey Area | Median Number of Employees, 1976[a] | | Median Volume of Construction Activities, 1975 (thousand dollars) | |
|---|---|---|---|---|
| | Nonunion | Union | Nonunion | Union |
| *Atlanta* | | | | |
| Residential | 6 | * | 389 | 500 |
| Heavy and highway | 18 | * | 875 | 5,000 |
| Commercial/indust./other | 11 | 24 | 560 | 2,042 |
| *Baltimore* | | | | |
| Residential | 6 | 5 | 296 | 500 |
| Heavy and highway | 18 | 75 | 1,000 | 5,000 |
| Commercial/indust./other | 15 | 25 | 464 | 1,750 |
| *Boston* | | | | |
| Residential | 4 | 9 | 169 | 750 |
| Heavy and highway | 30 | 25 | 633 | 2,077 |
| Commercial/indust./other | 8 | 19 | 364 | 971 |
| *Denver/Boulder* | | | | |
| Residential | 9 | 7 | 405 | 875 |
| Heavy and highway | 13 | 75 | 450 | 5,000 |
| Commercial/indust./other | 9 | 19 | 453 | 1,370 |
| *Grand Rapids* | | | | |
| Residential | 6 | 7 | 277 | 400 |
| Heavy and highway | 18 | 37 | 1,000 | 4,333 |
| Commercial/indust./other | 10 | 20 | 464 | 854 |

| | | | | |
|---|---|---|---|---|
| *Kansas City* | | | | |
| Residential | 4 | 7 | 189 | 389 |
| Heavy and Highway | * | 21 | * | 1,667 |
| Commercial/indust./other | 9 | 17 | 300 | 857 |
| *New Orleans* | | | | |
| Residential | 5 | 30 | 376 | 100 |
| Heavy and highway | 44 | 50 | 3,666 | 5,000 |
| Commercial/indust./other | 19 | 25 | 731 | 2,500 |
| *Portland* | | | | |
| Residential | 4 | 7 | 311 | 396 |
| Heavy and highway | 14 | 24 | 2,000 | 2,857 |
| Commercial/indust./other | 8 | 19 | 460 | 905 |

Source: 1976 survey by the Department of Housing and Urban Development and the Massachusetts Institute of Technology.

[a]Field employees on payroll in the fall of 1976.

volume of nearly half a million dollars. Union firms doing similar construction had a median of twenty-five field employees and a volume of $1,750,000. Given these general contrasts, it is still evident that there are a considerable number of large open-shop firms in all of the cities studied. Although, within just the commercial and industrial sector in all eight metropolitan areas, open-shop firms were concentrated among those firms with less than ten field employees, there were at least a few firms in most areas which were as large as the major union companies (see table 2-4).

For the United States as a whole, information compiled by *Engineering News-Record* (ENR) can also be used to characterize the relative size of open-shop firms. Every year ENR surveys U.S. construction firms to establish the "Top 400" in terms of volume. The 400 firms which comprise that list represent the universe of the largest industrial and commercial concerns, as well as heavy and highway builders. Most firms are general contractors, although major subcontractors are well represented. The number of open-shop firms by decile in that survey is compared for 1969 and 1979 in table 2-5. While the 51 or so open-shop firms on that 1979 list (the count is not exact because of dual-shop operations) are only 13 percent of the total,

**Table 2-4**

**Union and Open-Shop Commercial-Industrial Construction Firms: Size Distribution by Number of Field Employees, 1976**

|  | Number of Employees | | | | | |
|---|---|---|---|---|---|---|
|  | 1-5 | 6-10 | 11-25 | 26-50 | 51-75 | over 75 |
| Open-Shop Commercial-Industrial Firms | | | | | | |
| *General Contractors* | | | | | | |
| Number of Firms (236) | 47 | 62 | 78 | 35 | 6 | 8 |
| Relative Frequency (*percent*) | 20 | 26 | 33 | 15 | 3 | 3 |
| *Subcontractors* | | | | | | |
| Number of Firms (305) | 80 | 80 | 99 | 35 | 6 | 5 |
| Relative Frequency (*percent*) | 26 | 26 | 32 | 12 | 2 | 2 |
| Union Commerical-Industrial Firms | | | | | | |
| *General Contractors* | | | | | | |
| Number of Firms (269) | 24 | 44 | 71 | 49 | 30 | 51 |
| Relative Frequency (*percent*) | 9 | 16 | 26 | 18 | 12 | 19 |
| *Subcontractors* | | | | | | |
| Number of Firms (634) | 91 | 115 | 188 | 131 | 40 | 69 |
| Relative Frequency (*percent*) | 14 | 18 | 30 | 21 | 6 | 11 |

Source: 1976 survey by the Department of Housing and Urban Development and the Massachusetts Institute of Technology.

**Table 2-5**
**Number of Open-Shop Firms by Size Decile, 1969 and 1979, ENR Top 400 Firms**

| Decile | 1969 | 1979 |
|--------|------|------|
| First | 3 | 9 |
| Second | 2 | 3 |
| Third | 0 | 2 |
| Fourth | 1 | 6 |
| Fifth | 0 | 2 |
| Sixth | 3 | 4 |
| Seventh | 1 | 5 |
| Eighth | 1 | 8 |
| Ninth | 0 | 7 |
| Tenth | 2 | 5 |
| Total | 13 | 51 |

Source: *Engineering News-Record*, various dates.

they are well distributed throughout and are particularly well represented among the 40 largest firms. In contrast, in 1969, only 4 percent of the 400 were identifiable as open-shop firms and most of those were either relatively large or small. As a measure of open-shop activity this indicator is quite crude, of course, since either the nonunion or union general contractors listed on the ENR 400 could subcontract a major proportion of their dollar volume to either union or open-shop subcontractors. Nonetheless, the overall trends are indicative of the rapid growth of open-shop firms among the largest companies in construction. Yet these nonunion firms are still concentrated in the South: roughly 80 percent of the open-shop firms in the 1979 ENR 400 have headquarters in Tennessee, the Carolinas, Alabama, and Texas. Although many of these firms undertake projects throughout the United States, most of their work is still in the Sunbelt. Also, the growth of many of these very large open-shop construction firms has been stimulated by changes in preferences among large construction users. Major industrial firms, such as Shell, DuPont, and Phelps-Dodge, which had usually sought union-shop bids exclusively, now seek and support open-shop competition.[3] The most important reasons for this change are said to be, first, the increase in union wages and work disputes in the late 1960s and, second, the expansion of industrial activity in the rural South where union activity, both in construction and in manufacturing, has been weak.

**Relative Size of the Open-Shop Sector**

The difficulty of generalizing about the extent of open-shop activity, even when its rapid growth is apparent, is made clear by the data in table 2-6. Over the eight metropolitan areas, the proportion of nonunion employment

**Table 2-6**
**Union and Open-Shop Employment Distribution by Metropolitan Area and Product Market, 1976 Survey**

| | Total Firms | Product Market (percent) | | | Total Employment | Percent Nonunion By Area | |
| --- | --- | --- | --- | --- | --- | --- | --- |
| | | Residential | Commercial Building | Heavy and Highway | | Firms | Employment |
| **Boston** | | | | | | 28% | 15% |
| Union | | | | | | | |
| General contractor | 257 | | | | | | |
| Subcontractor | 276 | 11 | 72 | 17 | 12,980 | | |
| Nonunion | | | | | | | |
| General contractor | 107 | | | | | | |
| Subcontractor | 116 | 55 | 42 | 3 | 2,291 | | |
| **Baltimore** | | | | | | 43% | 47% |
| Union | | | | | | | |
| General contractor | 179 | | | | | | |
| Subcontractor | 216 | 2 | 63 | 35 | 4,246 | | |
| Nonunion | | | | | | | |
| General contractor | 151 | | | | | | |
| Subcontractor | 144 | 49 | 46 | 5 | 3,685 | | |
| **Grand Rapids** | | | | | | 37% | 20% |
| Union | | | | | | | |
| General contractor | 80 | | | | | | |
| Subcontractor | 77 | 1 | 48 | 51 | 3,136 | | |
| Nonunion | | | | | | | |
| General contractor | 48 | | | | | | |
| Subcontractor | 44 | 48 | 50 | 2 | 796 | | |
| **Kansas City** | | | | | | 12% | 2% |
| Union | | | | | | | |
| General contractor | 68 | | | | | | |
| Subcontractor | 146 | 7 | 61 | 32 | 6,624 | | |

| | | General contractor | Subcontractor | | | | | | |
|---|---|---|---|---|---|---|---|---|---|
| | **Nonunion** | 11 | 17 | 68 | 32 | 0 | 92 | 38% | 49% |
| *Atlanta* | Union | 130 | 177 | 1 | 91 | 8 | 5,884 | | |
| | Nonunion | 101 | 88 | 73 | 24 | 3 | 5,761 | | |
| *New Orleans* | Union | 82 | 87 | 1 | 92 | 7 | 7,162 | 41% | 36% |
| | Nonunion | 69 | 50 | 16 | 82 | 2 | 4,018 | | |
| *Denver/Boulder* | Union | 157 | 215 | 6 | 73 | 21 | 6,411 | 36% | 35% |
| | Nonunion | 110 | 98 | 67 | 30 | 3 | 3,464 | | |
| *Portland* | Union | 167 | 200 | 11 | 72 | 17 | 7,224 | 25% | 10% |
| | Nonunion | 69 | 55 | 66 | 24 | 10 | 784 | | |

in the sample of firms varied from only 2 percent in Kansas City to 49 percent in Atlanta. But even within areas with substantial open-shop construction, such as Denver and Baltimore, the proportion varied substantially by product market. In those cities the residential sector was composed largely of nonunion workers and firms while sample employment in commercial and industrial building was still two-thirds union. In cities where 90 percent or more of the sample construction employment was union, as in Kansas City and Portland, the open shop was concentrated almost entirely in the residential sector.

In 1973 and again in late 1976, and 1977, the Bureau of Labor Statistics (BLS) also undertook a wage survey of union and open-shop construction in major urban areas.[4] Comparing their findings for nine selected Standard Metropolitan Statistical Areas (SMSAs) shows that only two or three manifested major increases in open-shop employment during this period (see table 2-7). Those were Atlanta, Boston, and in particular, Washington, D.C. where the sample proportion reported as nonunion increased from 58 to 75 percent. While this time period is too short to capture long-run trends in open-shop growth, the BLS data does confirm the extent of open-shop employment in some cities, especially in the South, and the extreme variations in the size of this sector in different areas across the country.

**Table 2-7**
**Proportion of Construction Employment Classified as Nonunion in BLS Wage Surveys, 1973 and 1977, Selected Standard Metropolitan Statistical Areas**
*(percent)*

| City | 1973 | 1977[a] |
|---|---|---|
| Atlanta | 52 | 66 |
| Baltimore | 62 | 69 |
| Boston | 19 | 25 |
| Chicago | 1 | 1 |
| Dallas | 65 | 69 |
| Denver-Boulder | 29 | 24 |
| Los Angeles | 4 | 6 |
| San Francisco | 0 | 1 |
| Washington, D.C. | 58 | 75 |

Source: Computed from U.S. Department of Labor, Bureau of Labor Statistics, *Industry Wage Survey: Contract Construction, September 1973* (Washington, D.C., 1976) and *Industry Wage Surveys: Construction*, various cities (Washington, D.C., 1978.)

[a]Surveys for some cities were completed by the BLS in late 1976. Actual employment is not reported here because the BLS notes: "Estimates of the number of workers are intended as a general guide to the size and composition of the work force, rather than a precise measure of employment."

Similar empirical data for more recent years is not available. Yet there is no statistical evidence to contradict the impression that the open-shop sector has continued to expand. In 1979 in Boston, some major projects near the center city have extensive open-shop participation by general or subcontractors. In Houston, the building trades acknowledge that organized labor's share of construction has now dropped to almost 25 percent after having been over 70 percent ten years ago. And the Los Angeles area, where even single-family home building has always been completely union, now has the largest single chapter (over 550 firms) of the major U.S. open-shop employers association, the Associated Builders and Contractors. While these examples do not substantiate an overall increase in open-shop construction, they do provide some current illustrations of greater nonunion activity in geographic areas and types of construction which had remained largely union until the late 1970s.

### Subcontracting: Firm Entry and Specialization

One of the unique aspects of the construction industry is the prevalence of subcontracting. Construction projects are undertaken by a multitude of firms assembled for brief periods of time on a site and then disbanded. The variety of subcontracting firms is tremendous; although firm specialization occurs in parallel with union craft jurisdictions, subspecialties also arise around particular building components or technologies. Because of the amount of subcontracting in the industry, entry of firms into construction is relatively easy. General contractors can undertake projects of considerable scale without employing large amounts of direct labor or fixed capital; subcontractors can start with one or two employees and bid on only particular highly specialized contracts.

In the last twenty years there has been an apparent rise in the amount of work subcontracted. In a study of eight large projects in the Boston area in 1977, Machnik found that an average of nearly 80 percent of the construction cost was now subcontracted[5] (see table 2-8). Moreover, general contractors confirmed that a trend toward subcontracting had accelerated in recent years (see table 2-9). This was no less true in residential building where another study found that by the early 1970s, 68 percent of residential builders now subcontracted over half of their work.

The reasons for this trend are found, in part, in the changing nature of construction technology. Many building components, such as preframed windows and prehung doors, are now being factory-produced, delivered to the job-site, and installed by subcontractors. As this has reduced on-site

**Table 2-8**
**Work Items Subcontracted: Eight Case Studies**

| Project ID / Contractor ID | 1 A — Laboratory/ Research Facility | 2 E — Recreational Facility | 3 B — Shopping Mall | 4 A — High-rise Commercial Office Building | 5 C — Medical Research Facility | 6 B — Home for Elderly | 7 D — Hotel | 8 B — Nursing Home |
|---|---|---|---|---|---|---|---|---|
| General Cond.: Overhead | * | * | * | * | * | * | * | * |
| Fencing; Cleanup | ** | * | * | ** | * | * | * | * |
| Wood and Plastics: Rough | * | * | * | * | * | * | ** | * |
| Masonry | * | * | *** | * | * | | * | *** |
| Furnishings | n.a. | n.a. | n.a. | n.a. | *** | ** | n.a. | n.a. |
| Special Construction | *** | n.a. | n.a. | n.a. | *** | * | *** | *** |
| Doors | *** | *** | *** | * | *** | * | *** | * |
| Finish Hardware | *** | *** | *** | * | * | ** | ** | * |
| Equipment | *** | n.a. | n.a. | *** | ** | ** | *** | * |
| Concrete: Formwork Placing | * | *** | *** | * | *** | ** | * | * |
| Reinforcing | *** | * | *** | *** | ** | *** | *** | * |
| Thermal Protection | *** | *** | *** | *** | *** | * | *** | * |
| Wood and Plastics: Finish | *** | *** | * | *** | *** | * | *** | * |
| Miscellaneous Metals | *** | *** | *** | *** | *** | | *** | ** |
| Specialties: Toilet Partitions | *** | *** | * | *** | ** | ** | ** | ** |
| Other | *** | *** | * | *** | *** | ** | *** | ** |
| Sitework | *** | *** | ** | *** | ** | | *** | *** |

| | | | | | | | | |
|---|---|---|---|---|---|---|---|---|
| Finishes | *** | ** | ** | *** | *** | ** | *** | ** |
| Conveying Systems | *** | n.a. | n.a. | *** | *** | *** | *** | n.a. |
| Windows and Glass | *** | n.a. | *** | *** | *** | *** | *** | *** |
| Structural Steel | *** | *** | *** | *** | *** | *** | *** | *** |
| Moisture Protection | *** | *** | *** | *** | *** | *** | *** | *** |
| Mechanical | *** | *** | *** | *** | *** | *** | *** | *** |
| Electrical | *** | *** | *** | *** | *** | *** | *** | *** |
| Percent of cost subcontracted | 90 | 85 | 83 | 80 | 78 | 76 | 73 | 65 |
| Number of subcontractors | 50 | 10 | 15 | 34 | 51 | 25 | 36 | 25 |

Source: adapted from Nicholas J. Machnick, "Subcontracting in the U.S. Construction Industry," M.S. thesis, Massachusetts Institute of Technology, September 1977. Reprinted with permission.

Note: * = Performed entirely by general contractor; ** = Portions subcontracted; *** = Entirely subcontracted; n.a. = Not available.

**Table 2-9**
**Historical Trends in Subcontracting**

|  | About 1925 | About 1960 | About 1980 |
|---|---|---|---|
| General Requirements | G.C. | G.C. | G.C. |
| Sitework | | | |
| earthwork and site preparation | SUB. | SUB. | SUB. |
| site improvements | SUB. | SUB. | SUB. |
| water main service | SUB. | SUB. | SUB. |
| Concrete | | | |
| cast-in-place concrete | G.C. | G.C. | *SUP & G.C. |
| concrete reinforcement | G.C. | G.C. | *SUB. |
| Masonry | G.C. | G.C. | *SUB. |
| Metals | | | |
| structural steel | G.C. | *SUB. | SUB. |
| metal deck | n.a. | *SUB. | SUB. |
| misc. metal | G.C. | *SUB. | SUB. |
| Wood and Plastics | | | |
| finish carpentry and millwork | SUP. & G.C. | SUP. & G.C. | *SUB. |
| Thermal and Moisture Protection | | | |
| roofing, roof insulation, and sheetmetal | SUB. | SUB. | SUB. |
| thermal insulation | G.C. | G.C. | G.C. |
| precast resinous panels | n.a. | SUB. | SUB. |
| metal wall panels | n.a. | SUB. | SUB. |
| sealants and caulking | SUP. & G.C. | SUP. & G.C. | *SUB. |
| Doors, Windows and Glass | | | |
| metal doors and pressed metal frames | | SUP. & G.C. | *SUB. |
| plastic faced doors, transoms and panels | | SUP & G.C. | *SUB. |
| alum. windows and frames | | SUB. | SUB. |
| folding doors | | SUP. & G.C. | *SUB. |
| upward acting doors | | SUP. & G.C. | *SUB. |
| automatic entrances | | SUB. | SUB. |
| finish hardware | | SUP. & G.C. | *SUB. |
| rolling pass windows | | SUP. & G.C. | *SUB. |
| glass and glazing, alum. doors | | SUB. | SUB. |
| chapel sash | | SUB. | SUB. |
| Finishes | | | |
| gypsum drywall systems | n.a. | G.C. | *SUB. |
| gypsum board ceilings | n.a. | G.C. | *SUB. |
| ceiling suspension systems | G.C. | *SUB. | SUB. |
| acoustic tile | n.a. | G.C. | *SUB. |
| lath and plaster | G.C. | *SUB. | SUB. |
| sprayed-on fireproofing | n.a. | SUB. | SUB. |
| ceramic and quarry tile | SUB. | SUB. | SUB. |
| reshlient flooring | n.a. | SUB. | SUB. |
| painting | SUB. | SUB. | SUB. |
| vinyl wall covering | n.a. | SUB. | SUB. |
| Specialties | | | |
| toilet and shower doors/partitions | | SUB. | SUB. |
| toilet accessories | | SUB. | SUB. |
| cubicle curtain enclosures | | SUB. | SUB. |
| metal lockers | | SUB. | SUB. |
| access panels | | SUP. & G.C. | *SUB. |

**Table 2-9** *(continued)*

|  | *About 1925* | *About 1960* | *About 1980* |
|---|---|---|---|
| Equipment |  |  |  |
| hospital casework and related equipment |  | SUP. & G.C. | SUP. & G.C. |
| library equipment |  | SUP. & G.C. | SUP. & G.C. |
| waste compactor | n.a. | SUP. & G.C. | SUP. G.C. |
| dental and podiatry equipment |  | SUP. & G.C. | SUP. & G.C. |
| misc. equipment |  | SUP. & G.C. | SUP. & G.C. |
| Furnishings |  |  |  |
| carpeting |  | SUB. | SUB. |
| Special Construction |  |  |  |
| Conveying Systems |  |  |  |
| elevators |  | SUB. | SUB. |
| Mechanical |  |  |  |
| plumbing |  | SUB. | SUB. |
| h.v.a.c. |  | SUB. | SUB. |
| sprinkler |  | SUB. | SUB. |
| Electrical |  | SUB. | SUB. |

Source: Nicholas Jan Machnik, "Subcontracting in the U.S. Construction Industry," M.S. thesis, Massachusetts Institute of Technology, September 1977. Reprinted with permission.

Note: G.C. = General Contractor; SUB = Subcontractor; SUP = Supplier; * = change in party responsible for provision.

labor, it has also made the employment of specialized workers more transitory on each project. The general contractor is thus enabled to shift the burden of employment fluctuations to subcontractors, who can move workers between their projects, rather than absorbing the risks and costs directly. Machnik concluded, "Today, the general building contractor commonly retains only those tradesmen that he can continuously employ, and he is often faced with the option whether to employ any workmen at all."[6]

While the proportion of subcontractor firms does not differ significantly between the union and open-shop sectors in the metropolitan areas surveyed, the apparent growth of subcontracting in construction does have important implications for understanding the expansion of the open shop. First, subcontracting permits easier entry for firms as either general or subcontractors: the latter can be smaller and more specialized; the former need employ very little, if any, direct labor. Second, the number of tasks which can be subcontracted works to raise the level of competition in the industry. General contractors may obtain outside bids for any and all on-site work and the low bidders, regardless of union affiliation, may raise the prime contractors' profits. For these reasons, it is easier for open-shop firms gradually to gain access to parts of an industry which hitherto had been strongly union.

**Summary**

Although there is no doubt that the open-shop sector in construction has expanded rapidly in the past decade or more, there are no consistent data series which chronicle its growth empirically. Moreover, by 1976 the proportion of open-shop activity still varied considerably by geographic area, firm size, and type of construction. In general, nonunion firms predominated in residential, small- and medium-scale commercial building, and in some large-scale heavy and industrial construction. This has left union firms concentrated largely in medium- and large-scale commercial and industrial building and, in a few cities, in residental construction. By 1979, however, there are some signs that even these product markets are becoming increasingly open to nonunion competition, due in part to easier entry into the industry which is a function of greater subcontracting.

In addition to the compensation and work-practice differences to be explored in the following chapters, two other factors are important in explaining recent open-shop growth: rapid expansion of construction activity in the South as well as in suburban locations in general; and the drive and ability of many open-shop firms, particularly in the North, to expand beyond their original areas of specialization to capture larger shares of the market in commercial and industrial building.

**Notes**

1. U.S. Bureau of the Census, *The Census of Construction Industries: 1972*. Data from the 1977 Census has not yet been published.

2. Haber and Levinson, *Labor Relations and Productivity in the Building Trades*, pp. 252-253.

3. Interview with national staff, Associated Builders and Contractors, Inc.; also Gilbert Burke, "A Time of Reckoning for the Building Unions."

4. U.S. Department of Labor, Bureau of Labor Statistics, *Industry Wage Survey: Contract Construction*, September 1973; ibid., various cities, late 1976, early 1977.

5. Nicholas J. Machnik, "Subcontracting in the U.S. Construction Industry."

6. Ibid., p. 165.

# 3 Compensation, Skills, and Occupational Structure

Ever since the late 1960s, both the level and the rate of increase of union wages in the construction industry have been major issues of public concern. The last period of mandatory wage and price controls was specifically initiated to moderate construction wage settlements. Congressional debates erupt sporadically over the impact of the Davis-Bacon Act on construction wages and costs. The Business Roundtable, now one of the major private sector lobbies, grew out of the Construction Users Roundtable—an attempt by large industrial firms to develop better methods of controlling building costs. Currently, the emergence and growth of a significant open-shop segment in what had been a largely unionized industry has renewed attention to the union wage issue. Northrup and Foster (1975) and the Bureau of Labor Statistics (1976) have published extensive comparisons of union and open-shop wages which report union differentials so substantial—up to 100 percent in some cases—that the findings themselves have fueled political controversy. Unfortunately, because of problems in defining comparable occupations and skill levels, most of the recent research on union wages in construction does not shed very much light on the true dimensions of the union-nonunion wage differential. Nor do they consider whether, in and of itself, this is an important issue. In this chapter, two approaches to the study of construction union wage differentials are compared and evaluated: first, econometric estimates on the basis of individual worker attributes with, second, the 1976 survey reports of wages by occupation and type of construction work. The purpose of undertaking these comparisons is to identify the real significance of observed wage differences between union and open-shop construction workers.

Although one of the goals of a union is to raise wages and benefits, it is difficult to estimate the exact proportion of the increase which is due solely to concerted worker activity or, conversely, what the wage would be in the absence of a union. Figure 3-1 illustrates the reason for this. While a union may raise the wage in one sector of an industry to $W_u$, the presumed spillover effect of workers unemployed by this increase may depress wages in the nonunion sector to $W_{nu}$. Thus, the observed union-nonunion wage differential $W_u - W_{nu}$, may be larger than the "pure" union wage premium, which is $W_u - W_c$, where $W_c$ is the (hypothetical) competitive market wage. Alternatively, nonunion firms may raise wages in order to counter the threat of unionization and this action, by raising $W_{nu}$, will lower

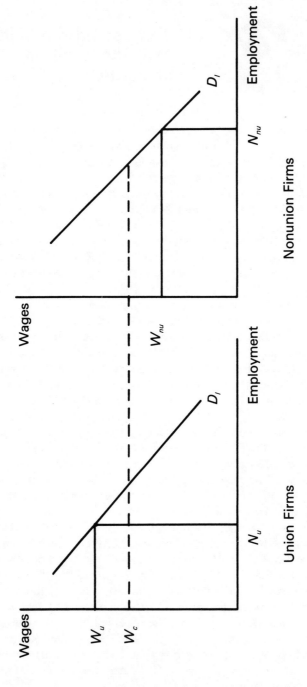

**Figure 3-1.** Hypothetical Union-Nonunion Wage Differentials

the observed union wage differential. As a consequence, the comparison of differences in union and nonunion wages says very little about the real impact of unions on wages.

The crucial comparison to be made is that between $W_u$ and $W_c$, the competitive wage in the absence of a union. This comparison would permit the accurate estimation of the amount, if any, by which a union raises the cost of labor above its market rate: the union wage "premium." But, because of the combination of the spillover effect from higher union wages, and the potential nonunion response, the competitive wage cannot be observed. In the absence of direct observation, replicating the competitive wage or estimating actual labor productivity in order to compute the union wage premium is a very complex task. Particular care has to be taken that the wage which is ascertained to be the underlying "competitive wage" accurately reflects the individual skills and productivity of particular workers under specific product and labor market conditions. In the construction industry, because of the diversity of skills, occupations, and product types, such rigorous wage comparisons are very difficult to make, as the econometric evidence in the next section indicates. As a result, tentative conclusions on union wage impact have to be drawn both from the comparison of overall union and nonunion wage and occupational structures as well as from the comparisons of final construction costs presented in chapter 5.

**Union Wage Differentials: Econometric Estimates**

Since the classic studies of Gregg Lewis (1963) on the impact of unions in labor markets, which focused on the union wage impact, economists have concentrated almost exclusively on the quantifiable effects unions have on this one aspect of the terms and conditions of employment. Studies by Oaxaca (1975) and Ashenfelter (1976), for example, have estimated union wage premiums for a cross-section of industries using data sets which report individual worker characteristics. Ashenfelter reports union hourly wage differentials of roughly 31 percent for white male blue-collar workers in 1975 in manufacturing and 49 percent for craftsmen in construction. Their basic methodology, summarized by Johnson (1975) in equation 3.1 consists of a single equation estimate of the proportional wage impact of unions, corrected for individual skills differences. Thus:

$$\log W_i = \beta U_i + \alpha X_i + \epsilon_i \qquad (3.1)$$

where $W_i$ is the wage, $U_i$ is a zero-one variable denoting union membership status and $X_i$ is a vector of all other variables beside unionism which affect wages, such as education, race, experience.

In estimating and reporting union wage premiums in construction, Oaxaca and Ashenfelter use this now-standard form of estimating the union impact on wages. The approach holds that an observed market wage for individuals is some function of the competitive wage, $W_i^c$, and a proportional impact of unionism, $\delta^{un}$, if the individual's wages are determined by collective bargaining. Equation 3.2 represents this multiplicative relationship in natural log form:

$$\ln(W_i) = \ln(W_i^c) + \ln(\delta^{un} + 1)\, U. \qquad (3.2)$$

Since the competitive wage, $W_i^c$, is unobserved, it must be replaced in the estimation by proxies. These proxies are observed individual human capital characteristics, given in a vector form $B_i X_{ij}$, and an unobserved noncompetitive impact of unionism, $\delta^{nc}$, which represents "threat" or "spillover" effects. Thus, equation 3.3 represents the estimating form of equation 3.2:

$$\ln(W_i) = B_i X_{ij} + \ln(\delta^{nc} + 1) + \ln(\delta^{un} + 1)\, U + E_i \qquad (3.3)$$

In the estimation, the competitive and noncompetitive impacts become subsumed in the constant term and the union impact is entered as a dummy variable. After estimation, the coefficient on the union dummy variable can be translated into the proportional impact of unionism on wages, all other things being equal. Oaxaca and Ashenfelter estimate this type of equation on a cross section of individual workers in different industries and occupations. To correct for the interoccupational-industrial impacts, they use multiplicative dummy variables for different industries and occupations, combined with common human capital characteristics (age, education, experience, and the like) as proxies for individual productivity. In other words, they allow for the fact that the constant proportional impact of unions may differ between industries and occupations. However, this heavy reliance on dummy variables is correct only if the error term of the equation is not correlated with any of the dummy variables. If there is any reason to suspect that the specification of the human capital proxies changes as industry and occupation change, then this estimation may bias the coefficient on union impact. In particular, if the standard human capital variables (age, education, job tenure) do not capture real differences in worker productivity, which may be correlated with unionism, as they may not in mechanical occupations like construction, then the specification error may positively bias the union wage coefficient.

To corroborate Oaxaca's and Ashenfelter's findings on the magnitude of the construction union wage differential, estimation of a similar equation was undertaken on the Parnes data file (1971) for older male workers. Since the estimation was stratified only for craftsmen in either the construction industry or in "other industries," no dummy variables for industry and occupation were included.[1] The results are reported in table 3-1. Two conclusions can be drawn from the regression results. First, the apparent size of the union wage premium in construction is substantial: 67 and 68 percent in 1969 and 1971. This is greater than the 31 percent premium for union craftsmen in "other industries" and is roughly consistent with the earlier regression estimates of Ashenfelter and Oaxaca.

But, second, none of the usual human capital variables are significant for craftsmen in construction; in addition, their relative magnitude is very small. In contrast, most of these same variables are significant, although only slightly larger in magnitude, for craftsmen in other industries. Most of this discrepancy in the role these variables play in the two equations is probably due to the fact that in construction, all craft journeymen in a local union receive the same hourly wage, regardless of type of formal training, education, or length of experience. Nonetheless, in both "other" industries and construction—and particularly in construction—these human capital variables play a relatively minor role in controlling for individual productivity differences. As a result, the estimated union wage premium—if it is correlated with any unobserved skill differentials—will be substantially biased upward.

In addition, at least two other studies have established that the estimate of the union impact on wages in the usual single equation form also may be biased by the simultaneous impact wages have on unionism. If, for example, unions organize or are found only in the high-wage sectors of an industry, as they have been in construction, then the causal interrelation between unions and wages may be difficult to unravel. Indeed, when Ashenfelter and Johnson (1972) use two-stage least squares to estimate the impact of unions on wages and vice versa in a simultaneous equation format, they found the impact of the union term, though positive, to be insignificant at conventional confidence levels.

While further econometric work may unravel some of the intricacies in the association among unions, worker productivity, and wage levels, major advances are likely to be prohibited by the nature of existing data bases. In most cases, the files that are now available on worker, firm, and industry characteristics are not sufficiently detailed to resolve these issues. Thus, in the construction industry, the standard single equation econometric test for union impact does not correctly control for individual skill differences and may overlook the simultaneity bias which comes with the internal composition of the industry, where the building trades unions have been associated

**Table 3-1**
**Wage Equations for Craftsmen, Foremen, and Kindred Workers in Construction and Other Industries, 1969 and 1971, National Sample**

| Dependent Variable | Coverage | Constant | Race | Area Size | Hours Worked | Collective Bargaining | Education | Occupational Training | Experience | Marital Status |
|---|---|---|---|---|---|---|---|---|---|---|
| LNW 69 $R^2 = .39$ | All | .9317 | -.2564 (.0480) | -.0266 (.0069) | -.9493 (.0518) | .2414 (.0367) | .0193 (.0066) | | .0018 (.0016) | .1562 (.1199) |
| LNW 69 $R^2 = .27$ | C | 1.4450 | -.5976 (.1462) | -.0549 (.0205) | -.3897 (.1802) | .5132 (.1190) | .0151 (.0218) | | .0048 (.0054) | -.1754 (.5144) |
| LNW 69 $R^2 = .32$ | C | 1.4016 | -.6247 (.1302) | -.0521 (.0182) | -.3103 (.1599) | .5728 (.1058) | .0129 (.0193) | -.0067 (.0038) | | |
| LNW 69 $R^2 = .31$ | O | .5474 | -.2737 (.0446) | -.0288 (.0059) | -.0555 (.1011) | .1239 (.0311) | .0292 (.0056) | .0020 (.0009) | .0061 (.0013) | .4170 (.1054) |
| HRW 69 $R^2 = .59$ | C | 4.394 | -1.75 (.224) | -.132 (.033) | -.227 (.285) | 2.08 (.187) | | .001 (.007) | | |
| HRW 69 $R^2 = .22$ | O | 3.048 | -.882 (.153) | -.098 (.020) | .756 (.351) | .339 (.107) | .117 (.019) | | | |
| LNW 71 $R^2 = .28$ | All | .9392 | -.2506 (.0383) | .0221 (.0051) | .1827 (.0603) | .2136 (.0278) | .0195 (.0049) | .0020 (.0009) | .0017 (.0012) | .3058 (.1156) |
| LNW 71 $R^2 = .64$ | C | 1.3416 | -.2701 (.0601) | -.0266 (.0085) | .0660 (.0640) | .5165 (.0503) | .0203 (.0085) | .0016 (.0019) | | |

| | | C | | | | | | | | |
|---|---|---|---|---|---|---|---|---|---|---|
| HRW 71<br>R² = .65 | C | 4.058 | −1.1855<br>(.2930) | −.1292<br>(.0417) | .0746<br>(.3123) | 2.575<br>(.0353) | .0923<br>(.0416) | .0049<br>(.0092) | 4.058 | |
| LNW 71<br>R² = .18 | O | .9396 | −.2387<br>(.0404) | −.0262<br>(.0052) | .0590<br>(.0845) | .1130<br>(.0284) | .0254<br>(.0051) | .0022<br>(.0009) | .0042<br>(.0013) | .2167<br>(.1065) |
| HRW 71<br>R² = .23 | O | 2.2175 | −.799<br>(.173) | −.094<br>(.023) | .594<br>(.362) | .349<br>(.122) | .110<br>(.022) | .010<br>(.004) | .0165<br>(.006) | .968<br>(.457) |

Source: Parnes, 1971.
Note: Standard errors are in parentheses.
LNW: Natural log of the straight hourly wage rate.
HRW: Absolute value of the hourly wage rate.
Coverage: C is Construction; O is Other Industries.
Race: Dummy variable: 0 for white; 1 for other.
Area Size: Discontinuous variable increasing from 1, largest metropolitan areas, to 9, rural areas.
Hours worked: Dummy variable: 0 for full-time; 1 for part-time (worked less than 35 hours).
Collective Bargaining: Dummy variable: 0 for "nonunion;" 1 if wages determined by collective bargaining.
Education: Years of formal schooling completed.
Occupational Training: Months completed, all types of occupational training programs.
Experience: Years worked.
Marital Status: 0 if unmarried, 1 if married.

with high-wage, large-scale commercial (or contract) construction rather than with the lower-wage, single-family residential building. As a result, although the econometric tests may confirm predilections about the presence and sheer size of the building trades wage premiums, they actually explain very little about their true cause and magnitude.

Moreover, the very form of these single equation econometric studies of union impact implies that unions are simply an independent, exogenous force which acts to raise the wages of an otherwise relatively homogeneous skill and occupational group. In construction, at least, the relation between unions, skills, and industry structure is more complex.

**Wage Survey: Union and Open-Shop
Construction Firms**

Construction is such a diverse industry that a survey which attempted to generate comprehensive new data on individual worker characteristics, wages, and productivity would be both difficult to prepare and prohibitively expensive. As a first step toward better understanding the role and relative status of unions in the construction industry, however, the 1976 wage survey of both open-shop and union firms asked for information on firm type (general contractor or type of subcontractor), product market (residential, commercial or industrial building), size (volume of contract work), and employment levels. Wages were to be reported by four different skill levels (working foreman, journeyman, apprentice, helper) within each craft. The craft names were left open so that nonunion contractors could use other than union craft designations. Wages paid in compliance with prevailing federal or state wage laws (such as the Davis-Bacon Act) were to be excluded: only "market" nonunion wages were to be reported. Finally, a specific geographic area was designated on a map as the reporting area: usually this was the equivalent of a metropolitan area defined by the SMSA.

Previous research studies on construction wages, by Northrup and Foster and by the Bureau of Labor Statistics cited earlier, have also used firms as the unit of observation, but they reported only limited information on firm size, type of construction, occupational definition or skill level of workers, hourly benefits, and the like. More important, because of the complexity of the construction industry, skills and wages of workers nominally described as "carpenters" or "ironworkers" may vary considerably within one occupational classification. Since the open-shop sector of construction is not formally constrained by the skill hierarchy and jurisdictions of the craft unions, similarities in job titles, such as "journeyman plumber," may also conceal wide variations in skill level and job content. Thus, surveys which only present gross comparisons between average union and nonunion construction wage rates by occupation fail to reveal much about the causes of any observed union wage differential. If, in actuality, the wage, job content, and skill level vary simultaneously between union and nonunion occupations in construction, the survey instrument must be designed to report these differences. For this reason, the 1976 survey was designed to capture, as much as possible, differences in both the wage and occupational structure across different types of construction for both union and open-shop firms.

*Skill and Occupational Definition*

In both the mail wage survey and in the contractor interviews, open-shop firms were asked to provide their own occupational titles or definitions. A representative listing of these for several union and nonunion occupations is given in table 3-2. For the most part the survey found that open-shop occupational titles reflected a narrower job definition than that contained in formal union jurisdictions. For example, while union journeymen carpenters are expected to be able to frame houses and build stairs as well as hang drywall, open-shop carpenters usually were listed as narrow specialists: "rough carpenter" (usually a form-builder for cement work) or

**Table 3-2**
**Union and Open-Shop Occupational Titles: Examples**

| *Union* | *Open Shop* |
| --- | --- |
| *Carpenter* | *Carpenter* |
| Carpenter | Rough carpenter |
| Floorlayer | Formsetter |
| Drywall | Sheetrock finisher |
| | Drywall nailer |
| | Drywall taper |
| | Framer |
| | Finish carpenter |
| | Carpet layer carpenter |
| *Sheetmetal* | *Sheetmetal* |
| Sheetmetal worker | Sheetmetal |
| | Heating and air conditioning worker |
| | Refrigeration mechanic |
| | Aluminum siding mechanic |
| | Furnace installer |
| | Welder |
| | Duct installer |

Source: 1976 survey by the Department of Housing and Urban Development and the Massachusetts Institute of Technology.

"drywall taper." To complicate the issue, however, the survey and contractor interviews also found that open-shop occupations can be broader than, narrower than, or virtually identical to the formal definitions of union occupations (defined by apprenticeship curricula and trade jurisdictions). In addition, some union journeymen in most trades, although paid a common hourly rate, have skills which are greater than or substantially less than the norm for a "journeyman." In many areas, for example, some union carpenters do nothing but hang drywall and are thus, informally, very specialized. As a consequence, without detailed information on the skills and productivity of each individual worker, union-nonunion wage comparisons can give only a rough indication of pure union wage premiums.

In the nonunion sector, broader occupations were most often found in general or heavy and highway construction firms. These contractors could define a new occupation, such as "general building mechanic," to do anything on a project site that particular subcontractors did not do. Given the large amount of work that is (or can be) subcontracted, some general contractors have become more project managers than large-scale employers of direct labor. New occupations, like general building mechanic, fit this role. In addition, a few large open-shop subcontractors are so diversified—especially in plumbing and heating-ventilating-air conditioning work—that they find it useful to cross-train mechanics in several skills or trades. This permits them to move workers around in the firm as demand dictates as well as help ensure steady employment for their work force.

In terms of skill levels, the survey results also established the importance of semiskilled mechanics or helpers in the work force of open-shop firms. Most open-shop firms pay a range of hourly wages (and benefits) to a group of workers they generally classify as "journeymen" or "craftsmen" and then another, lower, range of wages to workers classified as "helpers." Some of these helpers are informal apprentices; others are simply semiskilled workers. Helpers are used for much of the routine preparation, assembly, or finishing work on construction sites. Union jurisdictional rules or limitations on the number of apprentices usually prevent this substitution of lower-wage labor for skilled workers on union projects.

Finally, the union and open-shop sectors represent two different attitudes toward labor mobility and wage policy in firms. With significant exceptions, particularly among subcontractors, the union construction labor market is characterized by the rotation of a pool of skilled journeymen through temporary employment in many firms and projects. This labor market has a clear, common occupational structure (defined by both jurisdictions and subcontractor specialization), a rigid skill demarcation (defined by journeyman or apprenticeship status), and a standard wage and benefit level. The nonunion construction labor market is typified by smaller firms employing a mix of skilled and semiskilled workers often in firm-specific occupations at varying wages. Union firms, contractually obligated to pay a fixed hourly rate, try to manage the quality of their work force to ensure efficient production. The interviews found that, by and large, union firms were free to recruit and hire the best union journeymen and fire the most unproductive. They, in effect, tried to adjust worker quality to fit the wage. In contrast, the open-shop policy was to pay a mechanic "what he was worth." Most open-shop firms adjusted the wage to fit their particular criteria of individual skill and productivity. As a result, most paid a range of individual wages to their different craftsmen, although some others adopted a policy of uniform wages for different skill grades. While neither of these union or open-shop wage policies is necessarily better than the other, the union approach may be better suited to a labor market environment where numerous workers continually move between firms. The open-shop approach, where it varies wage levels individually, reflects the needs of a very heterogeneous group of firms that want the freedom to create a wage, skill, and occupational structure to fit their own particular construction specialization.

*Wage Dispersion*

The heterogeneity of skills and occupational variation of open-shop workers is reflected in the range of hourly wages (excluding benefits) paid even within one common skill-occupational group. Table 3-3 includes representative data on wages for foremen, journeymen, helpers, and apprentices in two metropolitan areas: Baltimore and Denver-Boulder. One source of this variation is that these tables report wages for one occupation but over all types of construction and sizes of firms. Nonetheless, the data show the tremendous diversity in hourly earnings for open-shop foremen, journeymen, helpers, and apprentices as well as the substantial overlap in the wage distribution for each of these skill categories.

Each occupational wage distribution also has an asterisk within it signifying the increment containing the local union hourly wage rate (excluding benefits). In almost all cases, the upper tail of the open-shop distribution overlaps the union rate. In some instances, up to 10 percent of the sample of open-shop workers receive wages comparable to union rates. Whether this comparability is due to competitive labor market pressures (signifying comparable skills for these open-shop journeymen), a "threat effect" of high union wages which pull up some wages in the local labor market, or the influence of prevailing wage laws is unknown. (Contractors were asked *not* to report any wages set by prevailing wage laws.)

## Table 3-3
## Occupational Wage Dispersion, Baltimore and Denver

| | Number of Firms | Number of Workers | $2.50-2.99 | $3.00-3.99 | $4.00-4.00 | $5.00-5.99 | $6.00-6.99 | $7.00-7.99 | $8.00-8.99 | $9.00-9.99 | $10.00-10.99 | $11.00-11.99 | $12.00-12.99 | $13.00-13.99 | $14.00-20.00 |
|---|---|---|---|---|---|---|---|---|---|---|---|---|---|---|---|
| **Baltimore** | | | | | | | | | | | | | | | |
| *Bricklayer* | | | | | | | | | | | | | | | |
| Foreman | 53 | 144 | | | 7 | 28 | 32 | 24 | 30 | 4* | 6 | | | | 2 |
| Journeyman | 56 | 254 | | | 30 | 30 | 56 | 44 | 44 | 46 | 4 | | 1 | | |
| Apprentice | 25 | 45 | | 6 | 14 | 13 | 7 | 2 | 2 | 1 | | | | | |
| Helper | 43 | 214 | 5 | 73 | 70 | 33 | 31 | | 2 | | | | | | |
| *Carpenter* | | | | | | | | | | | | | | | |
| Foreman | 102 | 234 | | | 3 | 23 | 80 | 67 | 30 | 10* | 12 | | 6 | | 2 |
| Journeyman | 93 | 457 | | 8 | 50 | 95 | 180 | 70 | 38 | 4 | 12 | | | 1 | |
| Apprentice | 32 | 83 | 6 | 30 | 31 | 19 | 3 | | | | | | | | |
| Helper | 70 | 433 | | 78 | 102 | 246 | 1 | | | | | | | | |
| *Electrician* | | | | | | | | | | | | | | | |
| Foreman | 34 | 111 | | 1 | 1 | 6 | 27 | 33 | 14 | 18 | 7* | | | | |
| Journeyman | 34 | 235 | 10 | 25 | 17 | 73 | 78 | 24 | 20 | 9 | 11 | 5 | | | |
| Apprentice | 30 | 103 | 9 | 26 | 38 | 13 | 8 | 7 | 1 | 1 | | 2 | | | |
| Helper | 21 | 89 | | | 40 | 5 | | 9 | | | | | | | |
| *Plumber* | | | | | | | | | | | | | | | |
| Foreman | 29 | 76 | | 2 | 1 | 12 | 23 | 17 | 11 | 7 | 2* | | | | 1 |
| Journeyman | 35 | 201 | 9 | 2 | 18 | 77 | 73 | 11 | 8 | 7 | 3 | 2 | | | |
| Apprentice | 27 | 162 | 11 | 47 | 82 | 18 | 4 | | 2 | | | | | | |
| Helper | 27 | 95 | | 43 | 22 | 14 | 2 | 1 | 2 | | | | | | |
| *Laborer* | | | | | | | | | | | | | | | |
| Foreman | 38 | 171 | 3 | 36 | 70 | 34 | 16 | 6* | 3 | | | 3 | | | |
| Journeyman | 27 | 229 | 3 | 49 | 139 | 33 | 1 | 4 | | | | | | | |
| Apprentice | 7 | 17 | | 7 | 10 | | | | | | | | | | |
| Helper | 14 | 135 | 5 | 49 | 61 | 20 | | | | | | | | | |

**Denver-Boulder**

|  |  |  |  |  |  |  |  |  |  |  |  |  |  |
|---|---|---|---|---|---|---|---|---|---|---|---|---|---|
| *Bricklayer* |  |  |  |  |  |  |  |  |  |  |  |  |  |
| Foreman | 16 | 29 |  |  |  |  | 5 | 5 | 2 | 5 | 12* |  |  |
| Journeyman | 20 | 84 |  | 15 | 1 | 11 | 20 | 19 | 21 | 5 |  |  |  |
| Apprentice | 14 | 47 |  | 6 | 3 | 21 | 7 |  |  | 1 |  |  |  |
| Helper | 10 | 44 |  |  | 21 | 12 |  | 5 |  |  |  |  |  |
| *Carpenter* |  |  |  |  |  |  |  |  |  |  |  |  |  |
| Foreman | 77 | 209 |  | 1 | 1 | 13 | 57 | 58 | 47 | 15* | 12 |  |  |
| Journeyman | 82 | 703 |  | 13 | 128 | 161 | 192 | 133 | 71 | 3 | 2 |  |  |
| Apprentice | 47 | 285 | 9 | 56 | 134 | 78 | 14 | 3 |  |  |  |  |  |
| Helper | 38 | 154 |  | 71 | 65 | 4 | 5 |  |  |  |  |  |  |
| *Electrician* |  |  |  |  |  |  |  |  |  |  |  |  |  |
| Foreman | 21 | 35 |  | 1 |  | 2 | 3 | 13 | 8 | 4 | 2* |  |  |
| Journeyman | 17 | 47 |  |  | 2 | 4 | 9 | 19 | 7 |  |  |  |  |
| Apprentice | 15 | 33 | 3 | 4 | 16 | 10 | 3 |  |  |  |  |  |  |
| Helper | 9 | 24 |  | 6 | 9 | 6 |  |  |  |  |  |  |  |
| *Plumber* |  |  |  |  |  |  |  |  |  |  |  |  |  |
| Foreman | 22 | 57 |  | 6 | 1 | 9 | 13 | 8 | 11 | 2 | 3* |  |  |
| Journeyman | 26 | 99 |  | 9 | 15 | 17 | 18 | 14 | 14 | 5 |  |  |  |
| Apprentice | 15 | 54 |  | 9 | 20 | 23 | 2 |  |  | 4 |  |  |  |
| Helper | 14 | 83 | 1 | 75 | 7 | 3 |  |  |  |  |  |  |  |
| *Laborer* |  |  |  |  |  |  |  |  |  |  |  |  |  |
| Foreman | 37 | 126 |  | 11 | 26 | 23 | 25* | 4 | 6 | 1 | 3 | 14 | 5 | 2 |
| Journeyman | 33 | 211 | 2 | 82 | 50 | 41 | 27 | 7 |  | 2 |  |  |  |
| Apprentice | 16 | 57 |  | 11 | 25 | 18 | 3 |  |  |  |  |  |  |
| Helper | 17 | 132 | 13 | 92 | 13 | 1 | 13 |  |  |  |  |  |  |

Source: 1976 survey by the Department of Housing and Urban Development and the Massachusetts Institute of Technology.

Note: Asterisk signifies the increment containing the local union hourly wage rate (excluding benefits).

*Average Wages by Product Market*

The wage survey data can also be used to report average open-shop wages by occupation in firms specializing in residential, commercial, or heavy and highway construction. (A firm was classified as predominantly residential, for example, if over 60 percent of its dollar volume fell in that category.) Appendix B presents wage (and union benefit) data in the eight metropolitan areas. Occupational differences in reported hourly wages across product markets are evidence of what Dunlop (1961) has called wage contours. In a competitive labor market, these contours presumably reflect intraoccupational skill differentials which are correlated with product types. These differentials may exist in construction due to the nature of the production process: residential building, particularly of single-family homes, has become largely an on-site assembly process of prefabricated components. Labor skills demanded in this sector may be limited in comparison to those in large-scale commercial office and industrial building where unique structures are built to owners' specifications. However, other types of commercial building, particularly low-rise construction like motels, office parks, warehouses, and restaurants are now making extensive use of prefabricated components and modules. These reduce demands on both the quantity and quality of on-site labor.

In the open-shop sector, the average hourly rates paid in residential building are consistently lower (across both occupations and cities) than the rates paid in open-shop commercial building. In most cases, these wage differences by product market are statistically significant for both open-shop journeymen and helpers. Moreover, there are also apparent differences in wage levels due to firm size. As an example, table 3-4 shows median open-shop wages for four occupations in Baltimore by type of construction and size of firm. Notably, as these indicators approach "union" characteristics (that is, larger firms in commercial building) open-shop wages tend to increase. In contrast, union rates, where they are both bargained and reported separately by product market, are usually roughly comparable in heavy and highway and commercial work but markedly lower in residential construction. In the few cases in the eight areas where unions have agreed to a residential rate, it is usually quite close to the comparable open-shop rate, though it is not clear whether any construction actually occurs at this wage. In most geographic areas, only high-rise residential construction is done by union firms and the commercial building rate applies. Thus, another major difference between the union and open-shop sectors of construction is the diversity of open-shop wage rates across products and firms compared to the relatively uniform wage levels found among union firms and workers.

As the data in appendix B also show, the union-nonunion wage differential—even comparing just commercial building rates for jour-

**Table 3-4**
**Median Open-Shop Wages by Occupation, Product Market and Firm Size, Baltimore, 1976**

| | Home Building | | | | Commercial-Industrial | | | |
| | General Contractor | | Subcontractor | | General Contractor | | Subcontractor | |
| Occupation | Small | Large | Small | Large | Small | Large | Small | Large |
|---|---|---|---|---|---|---|---|---|
| Carpenter | 5.75 | 6.25 | 4.75 | 6.75 | 6.25 | 6.75 | 6.25 | 6.25 |
| Bricklayer | — | — | 7.25 | — | 7.25 | 5.75 | 7.25 | 9.75 |
| Electrician | — | — | 5.75 | 5.75 | — | — | 6.25 | 7.25 |
| Plumber/pipefitter | — | — | 6.25 | 5.75 | 8.25 | 6.75 | 6.25 | 7.75 |

Note: Small firms had eight or fewer employees.

neymen—is substantial, although it differs considerably across trades and metropolitan areas. While an arithmetic average of all the differentials varies by SMSA from 30 to 60 percent, at least half of the differentials for individual trades are substantially below the econometric estimates of 49 percent or more cited earlier. Yet, after attempts to control for occupation, skill level, and product type there are clearly still notable differences in union and average open-shop wages. (The inclusion of hourly benefits in this comparison would also widen the gap.) Exactly what part of this union wage differential is due to bargaining power rather than to other unreported skill or productivity differences is unknown. Because of the diversity of firms, products, and workers in the industry, the mix between these two causes (as well as others) of the union wage differential can never be made very precise.[2] Thus, no dramatic conclusions should be drawn from these types of wage comparisons alone. In particular, higher union hourly wages do not necessarily mean that all union construction is necessarily more expensive or less efficient—as some have been quick to conclude. Nonetheless, for union construction to be relatively efficient as well as competitive with open-shop alternatives, union wages have to bear some close relation to the actual productivity of the average union journeyman. Only then will higher output—in terms of quality or quantity of work—offset the greater wage. The extrapolation from hourly wage levels to unit labor costs in complex, however; it is explored in the sections that follow and in chapter 5.

*Hourly Benefit Contributions*

Union hourly benefits, which are largely composed of employer contributions to health and pension plans, are reported in appendix B along with the union hourly wage. For union journeymen, payments for these benefits are clearly specified in the collective bargaining agreement, sometimes to the tenth of a cent; they comprise a substantial proportion of hourly earnings, ranging from 10 to 20 percent or more of the base hourly wage, and apply to all union firms, regardless of size or product market.

    The benefit structure in open-shop construction is much more varied. Many employers do pay part or all of health plan costs; others may make formal pension fund contributions. In other cases, where these contributions are not made, or even in some cases where they are, the employer may have a profit-sharing or bonus plan on a project or an annual basis. This variety of both types and sizes of benefits in the open-shop sector makes comparisons with the uniform structure of the union plans very difficult. The wage survey simply asked employers to estimate their total hourly contribution for the journeymen and helpers receiving benefits. As examples, benefits are reported in table 3-5 for several occupations in the Baltimore metropolitan area.

**Table 3-5**
**Average Hourly Fringe Benefits, All Open-Shop Construction Firms, Baltimore, 1976**

| Occupation | Number of Firms | Number of Workers | Sample | | Range | |
|---|---|---|---|---|---|---|
| | | | Mean | Median | Low | High |
| *Bricklayer* | | | | | | |
| Working Foreman | 13 | 44 | .71 (.08) | .45 | .12 | 1.66 |
| Journeyman | 12 | 34 | .62 (.04) | .55 | .10 | 1.00 |
| Apprentice | 4 | 8 | .62 (.05) | .55 | .45 | 0.80 |
| Helper | 7 | 51 | .55 (.02) | .55 | .14 | 0.90 |
| *Carpenter* | | | | | | |
| Working Foreman | 29 | 64 | 1.01 (.08) | 1.00 | .12 | 2.75 |
| Journeyman | 25 | 98 | 0.61 (.03) | 0.55 | .12 | 1.02 |
| Apprentice | 5 | 10 | 0.38 (.11) | 0.15 | .15 | 1.02 |
| Helper | 17 | 244 | 0.42 (.00) | 0.43 | .12 | 1.00 |
| *Electrician* | | | | | | |
| Working Foreman | 9 | 39 | 1.33 (.10) | 1.38 | .54 | 3.25 |
| Journeyman | 10 | 95 | 1.23 (.07) | 1.01 | .25 | 3.00 |
| Apprentice | 10 | 40 | 0.90 (.10) | 0.80 | .20 | 2.50 |
| Helper | 6 | 23 | 1.08 (.14) | 0.86 | .45 | 2.50 |
| *Iron Worker* | | | | | | |
| Working Foreman | 2 | 6 | 1.17 (.30) | 1.68 | .16 | 1.68 |
| Journeyman | 1 | 1 | 0.14 (.00) | 0.14 | .14 | 0.14 |
| Apprentice | 1 | 1 | 0.14 (.00) | 0.14 | .14 | 0.14 |
| *Laborer* | | | | | | |
| Working Foreman | 5 | 40 | .52 (.05) | .63 | .16 | 1.00 |
| Journeyman | 8 | 54 | .58 (.00) | .63 | .20 | 1.00 |

**Table 3-5** *(continued)*

| Occupation | Number of Firms | Number of Workers | Sample | | Range | |
|---|---|---|---|---|---|---|
| | | | *Mean* | *Median* | *Low* | *High* |
| Apprentice | 1 | 4 | .18 (.00) | .18 | .18 | 0.18 |
| Helper | 1 | 2 | .26 (.00) | .26 | .26 | 0.26 |
| *Operating Engineer* | | | | | | |
| Working Foreman | 11 | 26 | 0.82 | 1.00 | .14 | 2.00 |
| Journeyman | 10 | 97 | 0.78 | 1.00 | .09 | 1.10 |
| Apprentice | 3 | 28 | 1.00 | 1.10 | .14 | 1.10 |
| Helper | 2 | 6 | 0.58 | 0.80 | .14 | 0.80 |

Note: Standard errors are in parentheses.

Because of the extreme variation in open-shop benefit levels, it is difficult to make general comparisons with union programs. Overall, for those open-shop journeymen in the mechanical trades who do receive benefits—a proportion which the survey showed may range from 50 to 90 percent depending on the trade and SMSA—the level of the employer contribution is on average roughly half that in the union sector (see table 3-6). But, again, the range is so great that at least some open-shop firms equal (or surpass) union benefit contributions. On the whole, these firms tend again to be the largest firms in the open-shop sector. Ninety-one percent of all open-shop firms with a volume of over $1 million report full or partial contributions to a group health plan for field employees while only 54 percent of nonunion firms with a volume less than $250,000 report such contributions. Even greater variations by firm size are found in contributory payments for pensions—which, of course, are uniform across firms under collective bargaining agreements.

The divergence in benefit contributions paid by employers in the nonunion sector also carries important implications for understanding the role of unions in construction labor markets. Obviously, open-shop firms can enter the industry and compete on the basis of lower labor costs if they hire some temporary workers at a flat hourly rate and pay little or nothing in benefit contributions. While such seasonal or temporary workers are also employed in union firms, the employers must make hourly contributions on their behalf to fund benefits that few, if any, of them will ever qualify to receive. In this regard, open-shop firms have a cost advantage. At the opposite extreme, many skilled craftsmen work full-time year-round for the same firm in construction. In the union sector, the hourly benefit contributions of these workers go toward the funding of health plans, for example,

**Table 3-6**
**Percent of Open-Shop Journeymen Receiving Benefits Reported on an Hourly Basis, Selected Trades, 1976**
*(percent)*

| City | Electricians | Carpenters |
|------|--------------|------------|
| Atlanta | 74 | 13 |
| Baltimore | 40 | 21 |
| Boston | 54 | 39 |
| Denver | 50 | 35 |
| Grand Rapids | 79 | 64 |
| New Orleans | 84 | 39 |

Source: 1976 survey by the Department of Housing and Urban Development and the Massachusetts Institute of Technology.

for all union workers who qualify. Since those who qualify often include journeymen who work only 600 to 900 hours annually, the contributions made on behalf of "full-time" union workers (those employed at or over 2,000 hours per year) help to subsidize a fund to provide benefits for those who work fewer hours. But in the open-shop sector, the employer contributions for year-round workers can (and do) provide benefits for those workers alone. As a result, the same or even lower rate of employer contribution can provide a higher level of benefit protection for some open-shop craftsmen.

To the extent that the construction labor market is characterized by casual employment—that is, the rotation of skilled workers between firms, with most workers facing equivalent risks of temporary unemployment—there will be an incentive for all workers to contribute to pooled funds which provide a common level of benefit protection once a minimum number of hours are worked. Yet if some workers, because of skill and experience, rarely are unemployed and if other workers, because of their mobility, work too few hours to qualify, there will be an incentive for both groups to drop out of the union pool. The permanently employed workers can receive benefits only from their firm; the transient workers may prefer higher hourly wages in lieu of benefits. This dichotomy appears to be evident in the benefits policy of many open-shop companies. It clearly stands in contrast to the union ideal of uniform hourly contributions for uniform benefits.

*Supervisory Ratios*

One of the hallmarks of construction craft unions is the bifurcation of the occupational structure into a high-skill group (journeymen) and a lower-skill group (apprentices). A separate union (laborers') is available for some unskilled work but, due to jurisdictional lines, laborers are severely circumscribed in their activities. At present, very few of the building trades have an unskilled or helper category internal to the jurisdiction. For the most part, apprentices play this role, performing routine or unskilled tasks, although their contribution is limited by the journeyman-to-apprentice ratios specified in collective bargaining agreements.

In contrast to the formal union apprenticeship ratios and near total reliance on highly paid journeymen, open-shop firms have a potential advantage in maintaining some flexibility in skill categories and ratios. For the most part, these "categories" are largely informal and are visible only by noting the differing wage dispersion in roughly defined skill levels such as foreman, journeyman, helper, and apprentice (see table 3-3). However, larger nonunion firms such as Daniels, and Brown and Root, have developed formal systems of labor grading within each craft category for their large industrial projects. Brown and Root, for example, has four grades of pipefitters, with different skill and wage levels, below the level of "craftsman." While these grades may be comparable to first- through fourth-year apprentices in the union system, there are two notable differences: there are no time limits attached to the grade and there are no fixed ratios between the lower grades and a craftsman.

Offsetting the open-shop contractors' labor cost advantage in substituting unskilled or semiskilled labor for skilled journeymen may be the necessity to provide supervision for those labor groups. Ideally, the union journeyman is both mechanically skilled and professionally trained to work independently on varied aspects of construction. Lesser-skilled mechanics, lacking training, broad experience, or standards of the craft, may require both assistance and supervision to work productively. This supervision costs money and may offset at least some of the gains from the lower unskilled wages.

As a result, there can be major differences between the wage and skill structure of union and open-shop construction. The difference in these structures might be said to represent two different ways of organizing work: one ideally focused on the broadly trained "journeyman" and the other on a finer, more "industrial," division of labor. Of course, there are no necessary or obvious implications of these differences in skill structure for the relative efficiency of union or open-shop construction. The trade-offs may be such, in fact, that the total wage bill will be equivalent: a larger number of both unskilled and supervisory workers in open-shop construction could be offset by fewer of both in union construction combined with more highly paid journeymen. While only empirical studies of costs of actual construction projects can confirm whether this trade-off (or "equivalent wage bill") exists, this attention to the entire wage and skill structure of both union and open-shop construction again signifies that concern with a single union wage differential is misguided. Union journeymen may in fact earn more per hour than nonunion mechanics, but at least part of this differential could represent embodied supervisory skills. In the open-shop sector these are not contained in "journeyman" and thus are not reflected in the wage but have to be provided in an additional number of foremen at a higher labor cost.

The data on skill ratios available from the survey confirm the description of potential skill and occupational differences described above. In their present form the data cannot be tabulated on a firm or project basis, so aggregations across all firms in one product market will have to suffice. For six occupations in commercial building in Boston, for example, the average skill ratios in open-shop work were 0.6 foremen to one journeyman to 0.7 helpers and apprentices. Similar results were reported for Denver: 0.5 to 1 to 1.1 (see table 3-7). These ratios can be compared to "best practice" estimates on the ratio of foremen to journeymen in union commercial construction. These estimates are roughly one foreman to ten journeymen, though practice may vary widely by type and scale of project. The ratio of apprentices to union journeymen is usually set contractually as one for every four or five journeymen employed in a firm. So an estimated ratio of skills in union work is: 0.1 to 1 to 0.2. Comparison of this ratio with the survey results on the open shop reveal the expected differences: open-shop construction employs both more helpers and apprentices *and* more foremen than union work. (For the impact of this on project cost, see chapter 5.)

**Summary**

Viewed in the context of the product and occupational structure of the construction industry, simple comparisons of average union and nonunion hourly wages are meaningless. Indeed, since wage differentials may be offset by individual productivity differences these comparisons are useless without any contrasts of total labor costs. Further, econometric attempts to control for individual skill differences when estimating the size of the pure union wage premium are suspect due to the nature of the human capital proxies which are often used for individual productivity levels. Only carefully designed studies comparing the total cost of similar projects built under union or open-shop regimes can further advance the analysis of the union wage impact on the construction industry.

What the field and survey research shows, however, is that since the entry of nonunion firms in construction has been particularly notable in substantially different sectors of the industry, wage and benefit differences reflect in part occupational structures suited to specific firm and product

**Table 3-7**
**Average Skill Ratios in Union and Open-Shop Construction (Commercial Building)**

| | Plumber/ Pipefitter Number | Ratio | Sheetmetal Number | Ratio | Bricklayer Number | Ratio | Carpenter Number | Ratio | Electrician Number | Ratio | Operating Engineer Number | Ratio | Open Shop Averages (six trades) Ratio | Union Average Ratio[a] |
|---|---|---|---|---|---|---|---|---|---|---|---|---|---|---|
| **Denver** | | | | | | | | | | | | | | |
| Working Foreman | 18 | 0.6 | 14 | 0.3 | 12 | 0.4 | 65 | 0.5 | 22 | 0.7 | 10 | 0.4 | 0.5 | 0.1 |
| Journeyman | 30 | 1.0 | 57 | 1.0 | 34 | 1.0 | 125 | 1.0 | 34 | 1.0 | 23 | 1.0 | 1.0 | 1.0 |
| Apprentices and helpers | 81 | 2.7 | 21 | 0.4 | 28 | 0.8 | 91 | 0.7 | 40 | 1.2 | 14 | 0.6 | 1.1 | 0.2 |
| **Boston** | | | | | | | | | | | | | | |
| Working foreman | 18 | 0.7 | 15 | 0.6 | 10 | 0.5 | 51 | 0.5 | 56 | 0.6 | 7.0 | 0.5 | 0.6 | 0.1 |
| Journeyman | 27 | 1.0 | 27 | 1.0 | 19 | 1.0 | 94 | 1.0 | 89 | 1.0 | 15 | 1.0 | 1.0 | 1.0 |
| Apprentices and helpers | 21 | 0.8 | 16 | 0.6 | 8 | 0.4 | 53 | 0.6 | 104 | 1.2 | 5 | 0.3 | 0.7 | 0.2 |

Source: 1976 survey by the Department of Housing and Urban Development and the Massachusetts Institute of Technology.
[a]Union ratio based on "best-practice" estimates. Actual ratio will vary considerably among projects, firms, and over time.

specializations. Among the strong open-shop sectors are specialty subcontracting (where small firms may pay lower wages to narrowly trained workers); large-scale, multiyear projects (whose stability permits a finer, more "industrial" division of labor); and small-scale, low-rise building (where new technologies of prefabrication reduce skills needed). Thus, to the extent the open shop has been successful, it has been not only because it may pay equivalently skilled workers somewhat less, but also because it can substitute less-skilled workers for many tasks and pay them commensurately lower wages. Equally—if not more—important has been the ability of open-shop firms to vary both wage and occupational structures across different product markets within the industry. The relative uniformity of formal union occupational, skill, and wage categories contrasts sharply with the great diversity observed in the open-shop sector. Thus, while the union goal of uniform conditions may be an important source of interfirm mobility for journeymen, as well as establishing some general equity in pay, it is a policy which is now being eroded by competitive pressures in different subsectors of the construction industry.

**Notes**

1. The composition of "other industries" was diverse, including bakers, compositors, engravers, metal molders, shoemakers, and upholsterers. The equation was estimated on the basis of the occupation "craftsmen" working in these industries in contrast to craftsmen working in construction.

2. Open-shop firms often claim that even if they do pay lower hourly wages, their mechanics earn more on an annual basis because of their policy of providing a full year's work. The wage survey did not gather comparative data on weeks worked, but some data from the Current Population Survey for 1975 do not show any major differences in weeks unemployed by union or nonunion status.

Many open-shop firms do, in fact, employ workers year-round; but this is also true of many union firms. Smaller specialty subcontractors, both union and open-shop, try to maintain a stable work force; larger general and subcontractors keep at least a portion of their (best) journeymen. Also, the degree of seasonality of employment varies by trade: in the mechanical trades year-round employment is prevalent while cement masons, iron workers, and some carpenters and laborers tend to have moderate to high degrees of seasonality. Moreover, there are not very precise figures on seasonal fluctuations in construction by trade or union status; because of the short hours worked annually by many workers in the industry, average hours worked tend to be low.

**Union/Nonunion Weeks Unemployed, Construction Workers, 1975**

|            | 5    | 5-10 | 11-14 | 15-26 | 27-39 | 40-52 | Raw Total |
|------------|------|------|-------|-------|-------|-------|-----------|
| Nonunion   |      |      |       |       |       |       |           |
| Number     | 69   | 45   | 11    | 68    | 21    | 20    | 234       |
| Percent    | 29.5 | 19.2 | 4.7   | 29.1  | 9.0   | 8.6   | 100       |
| Union      |      |      |       |       |       |       |           |
| Number     | 60   | 32   | 18    | 59    | 29    | 15    | 213       |
| Percent    | 28.2 | 15.0 | 8.5   | 27.7  | 13.6  | 7.0   | 100       |

Source: Current Population Survey data tapes, 1975.
Number not reporting: 4,500.

# 4 Work Practices and Labor Market Institutions

If any topic has generated more controversy than the level of union wages in construction, it has been the impact of union work rules and institutions (such as the hiring hall) on management and efficiency. Over the last decade or more, journalistic accounts of the construction industry have focused on "union abuses" ranging from "rigid craft separation" and "featherbedding" to restrictions on the use of new technology or prefabricated materials.[1] No doubt abuses occur, but there is little evidence that they are endemic. Previous research on the work practices of the building trades by Haber and Levinson (1956) and Mandelstamm (1965), both of which relied on widespread field research, did not find that restrictive work practices were typical or that, if they occurred, the unions alone were responsible. Haber and Levinson concluded that

> there can be no doubt that some of these [work] rules result in increased costs, impose restrictions on managerial discretion, cause some misallocation of labor, and introduce other uneconomic practices. In return, they also provide a greater degree of security to a substantial group of workers, establish safer, cleaner, and more desirable working conditions, and protect labor from the severe effects of a competitive underbidding of the wage level. Furthermore, it is at least arguable that the economic cost of these rules has stimulated management to find ways and means of improving its own efficiency and has stimulated research into methods and materials which would economize on the use of expensive labor.[2]

As part of the 1976 survey, interviews with over two hundred contractors were undertaken in eight metropolitan areas to provide current information on the nature and impact of work practices in construction (see table 4-1). Both union and open-shop firms face similar management tasks of hiring workers, assigning work, supervising production, and training mechanics. The purpose of the interviews was to provide a comparative perspective on how union and open-shop firms differed in their approach to these functions, while also controlling for firm size and type of construction work. Findings based on the interviews will be reported on five subjects: occupational definitions, skill levels, hiring, work rules and technology, and apprenticeships and training programs. Since each of these topics could be the basis of a major study in itself, the findings should be viewed as an attempt to report objectively on the behavior of some firms and to develop hypotheses on differences in labor market institutions rather than as statistically reliable profiles.

**Table 4-1**
**Distribution of Interviews by Type of Firm, Eight Metropolitan Areas, 1976**

|             | Union | Nonunion | Total |
|-------------|-------|----------|-------|
| Residential | 9     | 62       | 71    |
| Commercial  | 28    | 36       | 64    |
| Other (Heavy) | 51  | 23       | 74    |
| Total       | 86    | 119      | 205   |

Source: 1976 survey by the Department of Housing and Urban Development and the Massachusetts Institute of Technology.

Overall, two tentative conclusions can be drawn from the interviews. First, labor-management and labor market institutions in *both* union and open-shop construction vary considerably by product market and firm size. In many cases, union rules on jurisdictions, skill level, technology and work practices, hiring, and training are neither as inefficient nor as inflexible as they have been portrayed. For the most part, these union institutions help make large-scale construction efficient by organizing and maintaining an external pool of skilled labor for many firms to use. In smaller-scale union construction, work rules are often overlooked or adapted through loose interpretation to fit the context. While open-shop contractors have the presumed advantage of the "right to manage," subject only to the constraints of the labor market, many of their practices—with some significant exceptions—do not differ substantially from union operations on comparable work, where it exists. The major advantage of the open-shop firm is internal flexibility on the assignment and control of work. The major disadvantage is the lack of access to an external labor pool of workers with predictable wages and skills which would enable more firms to bid on larger-scale work.

Second, the growth of the open-shop sector has brought a convergence of structure and practice in many types of labor market institutions. Open-shop firms, working through employer associations, are creating and adopting hiring referral systems, apprenticeship training, and even common occupational classifications and wage rates similar to those found in union construction. To some extent this convergence is due to government pressure (for example, approving only "traditional" apprenticeship programs); in other cases, such as referral systems, it is due to the needs of the firms themselves.

Important innovations which still distinguish open-shop firms are first, the widespread use of helpers as lower-wage semiskilled mechanics, and second, the creation of new occupational classifications that cut across traditional craft jurisdictions for particular types of work. Other major open-shop innovations are the activities of some large general contractors in training and managing a more specialized work force for routine tasks on large-scale industrial construction. These large firms also operate extensive worker-distribution planning and information systems which permit them to move supervisors, foremen, and skilled mechanics among their projects over wide areas. In so doing, they act to "internalize" the casual labor market otherwise organized by the union hiring hall or business agent.

## Occupational Definition and Jurisdictions

While the work assignment implications of union jurisdictional boundaries are easy to document in their absurd extremes, since they may require stand-by labor to perform only small tasks, they are not always inefficient for the union contractor. Large-scale work makes them relatively efficient; on smaller-scale projects the rules may often be relaxed. In all cases, of course, the actual influence of formal jurisdictional boundaries on work assignment depends on the extent to which they are enforced by the local business agent or steward of the craft involved. Over two-thirds of the union firms interviewed reported greater flexibility in work assignment than was formally permitted in their contracts (see table 4-2). The most common major problems which arose over jurisdictions were not the formal rules themselves, but uncertainty over whether the rules would be enforced or whether inter-craft disputes would arise.[3]

### General Contractors

For the union general contractor the major difficulty with jurisdictions is the lack of fit between occupations they define and the firm's current on-site labor needs. Over the past seventy years, changes in construction technology have reduced the role of a general contractor to that of a potential project manager. Where the general contractor, with his own work force, used to undertake the construction of the foundation and structural frame of a building, the continual development of sophisticated steel and concrete technology has shifted the general contractor's main tasks to sub-contractors. As major buildings or other projects have become more complex, general contractors have increasingly engaged the services of specialty subcontractors for steel frame erection and even for the forming of concrete foundations and structural elements. As a result, the on-site activities of the general contractor are now typically confined to small tasks: "anything the subcontractors don't do." The details are incorporated in the "General Conditions" of their contracts with owners.

**Table 4-2**
**Union and Open-Shop Occupational Classifications**
*(percent)*

Do your workers cross trade lines?

|  | Union | Nonunion |
|---|---|---|
| Never | 29.8 | 17.9 |
| Rarely | 42.9 | — |
| Occassionally to often | 27.4 | 82.1 |

Reason for working outside craft (for nonunion firms only)

| | |
|---|---|
| Tasks related to main job | 66.7 |
| Overlapping work | 39.8 |
| During seasonal lows | 21.5 |

Do you classify workers along trade lines? If yes why? (nonunion firms only)

|  | Yes | No |
|---|---|---|
| Nature of construction work | 68 | |
| Union influence | 6 | 16 |
| Davis-Bacon requirements | 10 | |

Do you have other noncraft classifications? (nonunion firms only)

|  | Yes | No |
|---|---|---|
| General contractors | 30.9 | 69.1 |
| Subcontractors | 13.3 | 86.7 |

Source: 1976 survey by the Department of Housing and Urban Development and the Massachusetts Institute of Technology.

These include such items as site cleanup, provision of scaffolding and other safety equipment, and material warehousing. In addition, general contractors will do final rework or "punch list" items, including such tasks as painting, repairing plaster, and replacing damaged floor tiles and washbasins. For this work, the general contractor will employ carpenters and laborers, but the firm will also need workers with skills and freedom to work in other areas. Thus, in the area of general contracting, the craft occupational structure of the basic trades is, in formal terms, somewhat out of date, considering the changes in technology and firm structure. If jurisdictional rules are strictly enforced, union general contractors may have to have workers of several different trades on the payroll in order to accomplish a variety of short tasks. This is particularly costly when workers have to be employed for the entire day in order to be available for one or two assignments. Indeed, continual attempts by union general contractors to evade or bend these formal requirements in the interest of "flexibility" are a major source of jurisdictional disputes. But on some small-scale work, particularly in rural areas, jurisdictional lines are rarely policed or enforced. A union contractor's relationship with his permanent employees often also permits considerable informal crossing of jurisdictional lines.

In contrast, open-shop general contractors emphasize their flexibility in work assignment. All of the open-shop generals interviewed in the eight areas were relatively small contractors. Their scale of operations on-site rarely justified more than a dozen men specializing in the basic trades. While these workers often had occupational labels similar to those of union journeymen, they did a wide variety of other tasks. For example, carpenters would often do ironwork or laborers would work on painting if the need arose. Although labeled as a particular trade, the nonunion general often spoke of these employees as general mechanics who functioned as supplements or adjuncts to the subcontractors in order to facilitate the completion of the project. The blurring of occupational lines usually occurred for one of several reasons; most often, it was due simply to the variety of tasks that needed to be done on small-scale construction, where there was not enough work to support one or more full-time specialty craftsmen. Having been exposed to this open-shop variety, open-shop workers would tend also to pick up complementary skills in construction and use these when necessary to complete a day's work or a job.

Some open-shop contractors began to formalize this process and refer to their men as general mechanics composing a "work crew." The crew itself would be charged with a particular aspect of construction: pouring concrete footings in forms, for example, or erecting a small metal building. In the concrete footings example, many members of a crew would do all aspects of the work of five trades. In union construction, laborers and operating engineers only would clear, grade, and grout the site; carpenters only would build forms; ironworkers only would set the reinforcing bars; and laborers and cement masons would pour and finish the concrete.

In nonunion work, a contractor would use a crew doing little else except concrete work; crew members would know enough of each of the trade specialties to do the type and scale of work required. In the metal building example, the workers would be basically ironworkers, erecting the frame of a building and attaching metal siding and roofs; but they would also operate small cranes or do rough carpentry. As a result of this practice, the "general building mechanic" occupation was created, combining many of the skills of the basic trades, as was the "steel building erector," adding to the skills of an ironworker those of carpenter, roofer, and crane operator. However, the exact content or nomenclature used to describe these occupations varied by contractor. Some open-shop contractors were very similar in the wide variety of tasks performed by their "carpenters;" others were traditional in not extensively mixing tasks into new occupations. In effect, the contractor was free to create occupations as the nature of the project or the capabilities of his labor force permitted. Thus, the freedom of work assignment, coupled with the variety of tasks associated with different types of building, leads to a very fluid occupational definition. It should be stressed, though, that the occupations so far created are not entirely open. They are shaped by the particular product the contractor is constructing. Thus, occupations are organized around a product or a type of phase of construction: concrete forms, structural framing, metal buildings. This type of occupational flexibility is now being recognized by the National Labor Relations Board in the awarding of work in jurisdictional disputes. Two cases which went against the claims of the ironworkers on the grounds of "use of multiskilled employees . . . ," are reported in appendix 4A.

Among very large open-shop general contractors like Daniels, and Brown and Root, jurisdictional lines and on-site work organization are very similar to union work. Again, it is the scale of activity which supports the specializations defined as occupational jurisdictions. Nonunion general contractors like Daniels, and Brown and Root do not hire men classified as "general mechanics," nor do they tend to move men from craft area to craft area on a job-site. Rather, the large projects which they build will often employ hundreds of workers of one craft—such as pipefitters—who will do nothing but cut, fit, and weld pipe. Even though these contractors enjoy a complete absence of jurisdictional lines and can move workers to any small specific tasks when needed, they still schedule and organize this on-site work force using mostly traditional craft classifications.

The large nonunion general contractors do, however, report some differences from similar union general contractors. First, they can create one or two new occupations to suit a particular type of work. For example, Brown and Root constructs chemical plants which require numerous valves and instruments throughout the piping system. The company has developed a single classification, instrument fitter, to specialize in this work. Second, both Daniels, and Brown and Root report that many of the men hired as semiskilled mechanics for routine carpentry or cement work early in a project may stay on, be retrained on-site, and do routine electrical or painting work in the later stages of construction. Whether this kind of crossing of jurisdictional lines is unique to open-shop construction is not known, but the stability of demand emanating from one large project in an area makes it occasionally feasible.

*Subcontractors*

Among nonunion subcontractors, the lack of union jurisdictional boundaries has two contrasting implications. First, it can make very little difference because the occupational structure of the mechanical trades is defined by state licensing of electricians and plumbers and the usual structure of subcontracting almost requires a "mechanical trade" organization. State licensing boards define tests for construction occupations which reflect "traditional" practice in the industry; the structure of subcontracting also defines similar occupations in the mechanical trades. Thus, many open-shop electrical, plumbing, and heating-ventilating-air conditioning subcontractors are virtually identical to their union counterparts. However, the second implication of the lack of jurisdictional rigidity is that some occupational flexibility within the firm is possible. This can occur in two ways. First, it permits mechanical crafts to undertake related tasks at the discretion of the contractor. For example, open-shop plumbers often dig their own trenches for pipe—something they would require laborers to do on union work. Laborers or helpers can be used in open-shop construction to wash sinks and bathtubs or set fixtures, work which union plumbers control. Second, pipefitters may also do pipe insulation or other work in open-shop construction, something which is the province of another trade in union construction. Thus, the lack of rigid jurisdictions does give the open-shop subcontractor a greater flexibility to do ancillary work as well as being a potential means of stabilizing employment in the firm as demand varies.

## Skill Levels

In theory, union firms in construction have access to a labor supply having consistent skills and clear craft demarcations willing to work at a predetermined hourly wage. When these conditions hold, union contractors do realize significant benefits; they can estimate and bid jobs with advance knowledge of labor costs and availability. In most areas and trades, however, there are usually major quality variations in workmen at each skill level (journeyman and apprentice). Firms can adjust to these variations only by varying the time employed; the best journeymen are kept on permanently as foremen or lead men while the less-productive are released after one day's work (see table 4-3). For the union firm, formal skill ratios (between journeymen and apprentices) are also fixed, so that the firm generally cannot substitute less-skilled, cheaper labor on routine aspects of skilled jobs. Of course, this substitution does actually take place—temporary, low-skilled "journeymen" do less-skilled work under supervision—but this substitution is not reflected in the hourly wage or cost of labor to the firm. As a result, over 75 percent of the union firms interviewed felt that there should be a formal "helper" category for the trades they employed. Many also felt that some of the crafts, particularly the basic trades, should abandon the uniform hourly wage for a "journeyman" and adopt a system of labor grades with varied rates of pay for different skill levels.

**Table 4-3**
**Skills Levels and Classifications**
*(percent)*

*Union firms only*
Are your union journeymen equally productive?

|  | *Yes* | *No* |
|---|---|---|
|  | 18.9 | 81.1 |

Should there exist an informal classification, "helper"?

|  | *Yes* | *No* |
|---|---|---|
|  | 75.3 | 24.7 |

*Nonunion firms*
Do you employ "helpers"?

|  | *Yes* | *No* |
|---|---|---|
| General Contractors | 76.6 | 23.4 |
| Subcontractors | 81.4 | 18.6 |

Source: 1976 survey by the Department of Housing and Urban Development and the Massachusetts Institute of Technology.

The nonunion firms hire and pay labor on the basis of firm-specific characteristics of work. Consequently, a range of skills and wages is found among journeymen, helpers, and apprentices in most open-shop contractors (see table 3-3). In addition, these contractors are free to design and assign work to whomever they please; this often results in both the specialization of many workers as semiskilled helpers in the performance of routine tasks, and in different skill ratios among firms. Helpers and lesser-skilled mechanics also serve to bear the brunt of fluctuation in labor demand in open-shop firms. These companies, like many union firms, will try to maintain stable employment for their best employees while they hire and lay off helpers as their work volume varies.

Contractor interviews asking whether worker skill levels varied between union and open-shop firms and across different types of construction did not result in hard data, but a small survey of electricians in Los Angeles and Boston by Gibbons (1978) did confirm that the skill content of workers in residential and large-scale commercial and industrial construction is quite different. Gibbons found that

> several examples showing how residential wiring differs from large commercial and industrial wiring, should substantiate the need for a sectoral analysis of construction skills. Homes, although they have more circuitry than ever before, can be wired with romex. Romex is a plastic sheathing in which the ground, neutral and hot leg for a lighting circuit are combined.

The flexibility and lightness of the wire permits the residential electrician to "rope" in a house quickly. He basically needs only to drill holes in the wooden studding and then properly snake the wire through to each outlet box. A large commercial or industrial building requires an entirely different technique. Due to the nature of this type of structure, some of the electrical circuits are not covered by walls like in the residential sector. It is therefore necessary to enclose the wiring in a conduit for protection. This means that the commercial and industrial electrician must be skilled in the bending and cutting of rigid or thinwall conduit. And unlike the simple placement of romex within a wall, this conduit must often be attached to metal and block walls or even fastened to a very high ceiling in order to reach the lighting placements.

In addition to the differences in the difficulty of installing the wiring, there is often a difference in the amps or volts that might be carried in these circuits. Residential wiring is normally concerned with single-phase, 110.220 volt circuits which range in the 15 to 40 amp category. The commercial/industrial sectors also have these simple circuits, but in addition they have requirements for more powerful (and also efficient given the scale) systems for the operation of motors and equipment. The typical industrial building would require a three-phase wiring system with numerous step-down and step-up transformers to adjust voltages.

There are, of course, many products and techniques which transcend the sector divisions. All the buildings need convenience outlets and simple lighting. There are also just as many extremes which widen the skill-differential between the sectors. A marked example is the intricacy of the sensory devices which shutdown a nuclear power plant in case of a meltdown, versus the simplicity of the low-voltage doorbell of a home.

Gibbon's skill survey of individual workers confirms these observations. There is a close correlation between skills used in electrical work and product market (see table 4-4). While these data do not reveal any union-nonunion differences in skill levels within a particular type of construction, they do show again that statistical comparisons between workers' wages have to control for skills which differ by type of construction work.

## Hiring and Referral Systems

Under the terms of many building trades collective bargaining agreements, contractors are required to rely on a local's hiring hall or business agent as a primary, but not exclusive, source of labor. In a 1969 study of the terms of nearly three hundred local contracts, the Department of Labor found that only 45 percent contained clauses which required, for example, that "the Union shall be the sole and exclusive source of applicants for the employer," while 34 percent required only that the union be given "first" or "equal" opportunity to refer "qualified applicants" and 21 percent of

**Table 4-4**
**Coefficient of Correlation between Work Skills and Sector**

| Skilled used in last year | Residential sector | Commercial sector |
|---|---|---|
| Romex wiring of lighting circuits | .4283 | − .1475 |
| Wiring and installation of three-phase motors and equipment | − .2490 | .1429 |

Source: Michael Gibbons, "The Declining Role of Craft Unions in the Construction Industry," B.A. Honors Thesis in Economics, Harvard College, March 23, 1978, p. 58. Reprinted with permission.

the contracts contained no provisions on hiring at all.[4] Surprisingly, despite these provisions in union contracts, the contractor interviews reported very few significant differences in hiring practices between different types of firms, either union or open-shop. Union firms, both general and subcontractors, most often hired by word of mouth through their foremen or present employees. When they did hire through a hiring hall, they often requested journeymen by name, thus avoiding the personnel assignment function of the business agent. There were several exceptions to this "informal" approach to hiring, however. First, when many journeymen in a particular trade were needed for a project (or the project was in a different area from the main office of the firm), the union business agent or hiring hall played the major role in recruitment and referral. These were found by contractors to be adequate mechanisms to assemble large crews quickly. The only problem was the variation in quality, particularly in times of peak demand. One contractor said that at times of low unemployment the hall can only furnish "warm bodies" and not skilled journeymen; nonetheless, under the contract they had to be paid the full hourly rate. Second, in times of high unemployment in construction, the hiring hall is not needed. Men continually come to the offices or gates of projects looking for work and crews can be obtained through these men or through referrals by employed journeymen of friends who are not working. And third, when the contract provisions on hiring were strictly enforced, they could become a major source of inefficiency to the union contractor. This was particularly true in trades with many small local unions, such as the carpenters', where firms were required to hire workers from a local when working within its geographic boundaries. For small subcontractors who tend to rely on permanent crews, the need to take on extra workers or lay off their own is very disruptive.[5]

The hiring methods used by open-shop contractors are similarly informal and diverse. Most workers are hired by word of mouth through present employees. Some contractors recruit directly from local vocational schools. Others find that men come to the main office or gate. When larger numbers are needed, recruitment is supplemented by newspaper ads or by using a local employment service. As in the union sector, open-shop contractors also vary their recruitment strategies with the state of the labor market—in troughs, workers come to them; in peaks, continual aggressive efforts using all information channels are needed to find anyone remotely capable of construction work. In many cases, open-shop contractors felt severely constrained without access to a common labor pool. Some did not bid on larger contracts because of the risk of not being able to obtain enough men at a given wage; conversely, others reported they could not keep too many skilled men on the payroll for fear of not having contracts to employ them. As a consequence, many tended to follow a policy of "controlled growth," to ensure that their permanent skilled labor force, supplemented by temporarily hiring semiskilled mechanics, was not overextended. Some firms began to experiment with joint bidding on projects which were larger than either of them could handle separately. And, in several areas, employer associations have begun experiments in operating open-shop referral agencies on a centralized, multitrade basis (see table 4-5). Although these systems might come to serve the dual purpose of referring large numbers of workers to a contractor on demand and placing others when laid off by a firm, the agencies as currently operated are much more modest. They act simply to list jobs and screen and refer individuals on a fee-for-service basis.[6]

Since hiring occurs in similar fashions in both union and open-shop sectors of the industry, the overall impact of the union on referrals is much less than is usually assumed. The local union does play a major role in referral if large numbers of journeymen—particularly in the basic trades—are needed by a contractor, but otherwise is often relatively passive in the placement of individuals. (However, many of the mechanical trades, such as the electricians, usually run much more organized referral systems, including maintaining lists of workers available ordered by length of unemployment.) While union contractors had the advantage of access, through a formal mechanism, of a labor pool of skilled workers, they also felt disadvantaged by being subject to the very formalities of that institution when it was not needed or desired.

**Work Rules and Technology**

There is no question that at various times and places, various locals of the building trades unions have resisted technological innovation in tools or materials and have established unduly restrictive work rules or practices. Yet, the results of the survey, as of other field research, do not support the contention that this has been a widespread or consistent policy.

**Table 4-5**
**Open-Shop Referral Systems: Nonunion Firms**
*(percent)*

| Is a central labor referral service needed? | Yes | No |
|---|---|---|
| Commercial | 40.9 | 59.1 |
| Heavy | 53.3 | 46.7 |
| Total (including residential) | 28.6 | 71.4 |

In construction, the topic of "work rules" can be said to cover a broad range of issues: from formal apprenticeship ratios to the contractual provision of iced water on job-sites. Among the types of work rules not covered in other sections of this chapter which affect on-site productivity are those that

1. Fix regular hours of work in a day (for example, 8 a.m. to 4 p.m.) or regular days of work in a week (say, Monday through Friday) for all contractors;
2. Restrict the kind or amount of work performed off-site (for instance, in the shop of a contractor);
3. Restrict the use of tools or amount of work by a foreman or employer;
4. Require a foreman to be designated when a crew size reaches a given number; and
5. Require more than the necessary number of workers on particular machinery and equipment (for example, pump or elevator operators or limitations on the number of different machines operated per day).

Union contractor complaints about these types of practices varied by trade and by area. The operating engineers and ironworkers, particularly on the eastern seaboard, were reported to be particularly difficult over numbers of workers for given jobs; while the mechanical trades, again in the eastern areas, were most restrictive on work performed on-site. Union contractors in the South or West, had fewer problems with these types of contractual provisions. (They attributed this to the lesser market power of the union in those areas.) Even in the East the strongest protests over work rule restrictions came from smaller union firms or from contractors dealing with particularly militant union business agents. Overall, however, 55 percent of the union contractors interviewed reported no work-rule restrictions of the types listed; another 3 percent reported such contractual provisions but noted they were no longer enforced.

Even for union contractors directly affected by these types of work rules, their impact on efficiency differed considerably by firm size or the scale of the project under construction. Restrictions on an employer's use of the tools of the trade are irrelevant for multimillion dollar firms, for example, but they can be a considerable hindrance to specialty subcontractors which may employ only a few journeymen under the direct supervision of the owner—who is usually a former journeyman and often still a union member. Requirements on crew size or work distribution also rarely constrain large firms which undertake projects of a scale that can efficiently sustain the activity of many journeymen in one trade; but these same rules can produce featherbedding when applied and enforced on smaller construction contracts. Indeed, the very dissimilarity in effects of these rules across firms makes it difficult to sustain multi-employer bargaining coalitions to remove such rules from contracts. For the most part, the largest employers have had very little incentive to take a strike or support a lockout in order to eliminate them. Even if all employers within a local area were to agree on changes in some work rules as bargaining priorities, the geographical fragmentation of local bargaining may find them undercut by neighboring or national firms which did not share their objectives.

In contrast to the divergence of views within the union sector, all the open-shop contractors interviewed were nearly rhapsodic about their escape from all forms of work rules. All of these rules were perceived to be onerous restrictions on the "right to manage." In their words, nonunion status provided the crucial element of "flexibility" in assigning construction tasks. Although such flexibility had varied implications for firms of different sizes or specialties, the specific examples given by open-shop contractors all related to the ability to respond freely and quickly to the exigencies of a particular project, location, or technology. Since construction work is so heterogeneous, a contractor's freedom to vary worker placement, supervision, or volume of on-site fabrication can be important in controlling costs and in competing for work. Unions attempt to standardize work conditions through contractual rules, largely to constrain the ability of construction management to discriminate against individual workers. (Work rules do establish uniform conditions which can result in more equitable treatment of workers.) But the very uniformity of these rules creates a tension between them and the varying demands of on-site production. Confronted by the need to cope with a diverse range of production tasks in a climate of uncertainty, management flexibility in construction can take on an almost symbolic importance.

Work rules which result in restrictions on technology rather than on worker placement can take either of two forms: restrictions on materials, particularly those which are prefabricated or nonunion; or restrictions on tools, especially those which substitute mechanical aid or power for worker strength and skill. In this area, the differences between union and open-shop firms were not as pronounced as those apparent over some types of work rules. Ninety-two percent of the union firms interviewed said there were no restrictions on materials and 95 percent reported no restrictions on tools. The restrictions which did occur were not on prefabricated materials as such, but on nonunion prefabricated products. As one contractor commented, "As long as it has some sort of union label on it, it's acceptable." In contrast, the open-shop firms reported no employee restrictions on either tools and materials. While they again emphasized their freedom to substitute prefabricated or preengineered modules for on-site skilled labor, over 80 percent of the nonunion firms reported that they believed union companies also used similar equipment and materials.

These findings on the general acceptance of technological change in materials and tools in construction are consistent with other findings on the changing composition of building input requirements. In a series of studies in the last twenty years, the Bureau of Labor Statistics has documented a continuing decline in on-site employee hours per dollar volume of construction. This has occurred in heavy construction (such as dam and dredging projects) as well as in commercial buildings (such as office, school, and hospital structures). These declines are due not only to greater capital intensity of on-site operations (such as larger earthmoving machinery) and more off-site fabrication of materials and equipment, but also to shifts in the composition and geographic location of construction activity.[7] Recently, some firms have come to specialize in preengineered construction which relies on standardized structural components, produced in large volume, and on general basic designs common to many different building types and purposes. One major building manufacturer notes:

> Compared to conventional construction methods, pre-engineered construction requires less field labor, and factory fabrication generally means that the quality of a pre-engineered building is better. Closely related is another advantage: construction, owning, and operating costs of pre-engineered buildings are more predictable, helping to minimize and control the risks of construction cost overruns and design oversights.

> It has been often pointed out that the upward spiral of field labor rates has had a greater impact on conventional construction than on pre-engineered construction. It is also said that pre-engineered construction has an economic edge over conventional construction through its substitution of lower factory labor rates for higher field labor rates.[8]

What is important is not only that this type of technological change has occurred, but that its occurrence directly affects the level and composition of skills demanded on construction job-sites. To the extent that some construction evolves into an on-site assembly process, the traditional skills of many craft journeymen become obsolete. Skilled craftsmen can be replaced by semiskilled mechanics on-site and by machine processes in manufacturing firms or in the central shops of construction companies off-site. While this process of skill substitution is by no means universal, since larger and more complicated capital equipment and demands for high quality or tolerances may also raise skill requirements, it has affected a considerable proportion of residential and commercial building. It is in these types of construction where the particular occupational, skill, and wage structure, rather than a greater willingness to use new technology, gives open-shop firms a special advantage.

**Work Rules and Disputes**

One other important impact of union work and jurisdictional rules in construction is more a function of political structure than of contract language. The presence of unions on a job-site automatically interferes with a contractor's perceived "right to manage." Whether the building trades adopt formal restrictive practices or not, the union presence can always complicate any change management feels is necessary. Management's resentment of unions in construction (as in other industries) seems to stem less from the imposition of direct costs than from the potential uncertainty and perceived instability of union reaction. When interviewed, project managers and small contractors stressed the role of "politics" in determining union behavior. On one job-site, for example, a project manager may deal with six to eighteen different trades. Each of these may have a steward on the site; all will have a local business agent in the area. The temper of this union leadership in policing the agreements determines the flow of work. Contractors feel that too many work stoppages occur simply because of intra- and inter-union competition over political leadership. Since local unions officers and many business agents are elected and stewards may be running for office, their campaigns and their attractiveness to the membership may depend on how "tough" they are on management. Harassment of management even over—or perhaps especially over—minor issues like work rules apparently can play an important role in building a personal constituency. A multiunion structure in the industry not only expands the opportunity for this kind of political competition, it also makes the union sector of construction in a particular region vulnerable to minor disputes among numerous local unions. The resulting work stoppages or slowdowns, of course, have a significant effect on the costs of the union firms involved, and on their ability to guarantee project completion dates to clients. While union contractors are rarely blameless in even the most "political" of disputes, the resulting disruptions only increase the attractiveness of open-shop firms to construction users. Thus, even when the direct economic impact of work rules may be small, their apparent ability to generate work disruptions and stoppages—even in the presence of dispute boards and the like—works to the long-run disadvantage of union firms and workers.

## Apprenticeship and Training

Apprenticeship and training programs in union and open-shop construction exhibit significant differences in structure and approach as well as some substantial similarities. The open-shop sector does have a large number—namely twenty thousand—of apprentices registered in all of the major construction occupations and operates certified programs in nearly all of the continental states. (Certified apprenticeship programs are those approved by state apprenticeship councils or, in their absence, by the federal Bureau of Apprenticeship and Training; only those approved are eligible for government funding of after-hours classroom training and only apprentices registered in those programs may be paid at apprentice rates on public construction.) The majority of open-shop certified apprentices are found in three occupations—carpentry, electrical work, and plumbing—and concentrated in a few states such as North Carolina, Maryland, and Florida. In contrast, the number of union certified apprentices is substantially greater, more widespread geographically, and represents more trades.

Because of the operation of federal and state apprenticeship certification processes, the registered open-shop programs tend to be virtually identical to union programs. They follow the same occupational lines and have virtually identical curricula and time spans. Government agencies even require that local open-shop associations set common wage levels for apprentices in the same manner in which wages are determined in union programs: a certain percentage of the journeyman's wage for the first year; a higher percentage for the second year, and so on. Although at the national level there is no longer any resistance to certifying open-shop programs, as such, as long as they are in accord with "traditional" (that is, union) criteria, considerable opposition was reported to exist at regional federal offices and among state apprenticeship councils. This resistance has intensified when open-shop associations have tried to certify programs for new occupations, such as general building mechanic, which are (or might become) prevalent in the nonunion sector. In some states, attempts to certify such nontraditional occupations have led to lengthy court battles (in California, for example) or special bills before state legislatures (as in Oregon). Although government agencies will certify almost any apprenticeable occupation at the level of the firm in manufacturing or service sectors of the economy, there appears to be special opposition to innovations in occupational definition and training in construction. While this policy may represent the desire to unify standards across firms in a casual labor market, the practice deprives nonunion firms of government subsidies for apprentice programs and of the ability to use apprentices on public construction work. It also may account, in part, for the relatively low number of certified open-shop apprentices even in states which have a high proportion of nonunion construction workers.

### Minority Participation

Since the passage of the Civil Rights Act in 1964, a number of federal programs have been established to increase the proportion of minorities—and, in 1979, of women—employed in the construction industry. For the most part, analysis of the effectiveness of these efforts has focused on the union sector of the industry and in particular on the degree of entry and success of minorities in the formal apprenticeship programs of the building trades.[9] Recent data from a General Accounting Office (GAO) report critical of federal efforts to increase minority participation show, in fact, that relatively little progress has been made (see table 4-6). The percent minority membership in the major skilled craft unions increased from an average of 9.3 percent in 1972 to 12.8 in 1976. Although even these small gains did occur during a period of substantial unemployment in the industry, the GAO concludes that programs administered by the Equal Employment Opportunity Commission, the Office of Federal Contract Compliance, and the Job Corps have had "limited impact."[10]

In such public and academic discussions of the extent of discrimination against minorities in construction and the proper remedy for it, very little attention has been paid to the open-shop sector. While this is in large part due to the relative absence of data on minorities in nonunion construction firms, that lack has not prevented some from concluding that "the open shop sector is both more hospitable as a whole to minority employment and, being without craft restrictions and union rigidities, more capable of dealing with the problem."[11]

This conclusion is not supported, however, by the only available data on minority participation in union and nonunion apprenticeship programs. Since 1976 the Department of Labor has compiled national statistics on the number and type of union and open-shop apprentices in certified programs in each state.[12] Tabulations from that data show that minority participation, both in terms of percentages and absolute numbers, is substantially higher in union programs (see tables 4-7 and 4-8). At the end of 1976 and in June 1978, as examples, 21 percent of the apprentices in union programs were classified as minority; in the same years, only 10 percent of the nonunion apprentices were minorities. In both union and open-shop programs,

**Table 4-6**
**Minority Membership in Selected Skilled Construction Craft Unions between 1972 and 1976 as Reported by Unions to the Equal Employment Opportunity Commission**

| Trade | Minority membership | | | Minority underrepresentation gap | | |
|---|---|---|---|---|---|---|
| | 1972 | 1976 | Increase or decrease | 1972 | 1976 | Increase or decrease |
| Asbestos workes | 3.7 | 6.4 | 2.7 | 13.5 | 12.0 | -1.5 |
| Bricklayers | 13.1 | 13.9 | 0.8 | 4.1 | 4.5 | 0.4 |
| Carpenters | 11.2 | 13.3 | 2.1 | 6.0 | 5.1 | -0.9 |
| Electrical workers | 7.5 | 10.7 | 3.2 | 9.7 | 7.7 | -2.0 |
| Iron workers | 9.3 | 18.3 | 9.0 | 7.9 | 0.1 | -7.8 |
| Lathers | 14.2 | 20.6 | 6.4 | 3.0 | -2.2[a] | -5.2 |
| Marble polishers | 15.2 | 14.4 | -0.8 | 2.0 | 4.0 | 2.0 |
| Operating engineers | 6.2 | 11.6 | 5.4 | 11.0 | 6.8 | -4.2 |
| Painters | 14.8 | 17.8 | 3.0 | 2.4 | 0.6 | -1.8 |
| Plasteres and cement masons | 32.5 | 36.6 | 4.1 | -15.3[a] | -18.2 | -2.9 |
| Plumbers | 4.5 | 8.0 | 3.5 | 12.7 | 10.4 | -2.3 |
| Roofers | 23.4 | 22.7 | -0.7 | -6.2[a] | -4.3 | 1.9 |
| Sheetmetal workers | 7.0 | 8.9 | 1.9 | 10.2 | 9.5 | -0.7 |
| Total | 9.3 | 12.8 | 3.5 | 7.9 | 5.6 | -2.3 |

Source: General Accounting Office, *The Davis-Bacon Act Should Be Repealed* (Washington, D.C., 1979), appendix I.

Note: The minority underrepresentation gap is the difference between minority proportional representation in the craft and in the national population: minorities represented 17.2 percent of the national population in 1972 and 18.4 percent in 1976.

[a]The proportion of minorities in the craft is greater than the proportion of minorities in the national population.

**Table 4-7**
**Apprentices in Selected Joint and Nonjoint Programs: Total and by Minority Status, 1976 U.S. Totals**

| Trade | Joint | | | Nonjoint | | |
|---|---|---|---|---|---|---|
| | | Minority | | | Minority | |
| | Total | Number | Percent | Total | Number | Percent |
| Bricklayers, stone and tile setters | 5,714 | 1,272 | 22 | 544 | 68 | 13 |
| Carpenters | 28,102 | 5,323 | 19 | 3,236 | 389 | 12 |
| Cement masons | 2,413 | 1,110 | 46 | 77 | 28 | 36 |
| Electricians | 20,487 | 3,544 | 17 | 6,577 | 675 | 11 |
| Glaziers | 997 | 251 | 25 | 88 | 9 | 10 |
| Insulation workers | 1,812 | 372 | 21 | 149 | 22 | 15 |
| Lathers | 1,059 | 313 | 30 | 44 | 5 | 11 |
| Operating engineers | 5,516 | 1,725 | 31 | 160 | 33 | 21 |
| Painters | 5,324 | 1,274 | 24 | 207 | 73 | 35 |
| Pipefitters, sprinkler and steamfitters | 12,191 | 1,958 | 16 | 699 | 39 | 6 |
| Plasterers | 995 | 387 | 39 | 18 | 6 | 33 |
| Plumbers | 11,759 | 2,105 | 18 | 4,579 | 258 | 6 |
| Roofers | 3,814 | 1,271 | 33 | 211 | 18 | 9 |
| Sheetmetal | 7,227 | 1,421 | 20 | 1,176 | 119 | 10 |
| Structural steel | 7,199 | 1,508 | 21 | 96 | 23 | 24 |
| Total | 114,609 | 23,834 | 21 | 17,861 | 1,765 | 10 |

Source: Bureau of Apprenticeship and Training, U.S. Department of Labor. Unpublished data tabulated for this study.
Note: Joint and nonjoint programs refer to union and open-shop programs, respectively.

**Table 4-8**
**Apprentices in Selected Joint and Nonjoint Programs: Total and by Minority Status, 1978 U.S. Totals**

| | Joint | | | Nonjoint | | |
|---|---|---|---|---|---|---|
| | *Total* | *Minorities* | *Percent* | *Total* | *Minorities* | *Percent* |
| Bricklayers | 6,768 | 1,574 | 23.3 | 650 | 124 | 19.1 |
| Carpenters | 31,191 | 5,941 | 19.0 | 3,438 | 474 | 13.8 |
| Cement masons | 2,513 | 1,184 | 47.1 | 88 | 40 | 45.5 |
| Electricians | 19,330 | 3,325 | 17.2 | 6,887 | 746 | 10.8 |
| Floor coverers | 1,230 | 277 | 22.5 | 80 | 10 | 12.5 |
| Glaziers | 903 | 194 | 21.5 | 98 | 9 | 9.2 |
| Insulation workers | 1,807 | 426 | 23.6 | 196 | 37 | 18.8 |
| Lathers | 1,210 | 348 | 28.8 | 41 | 4 | 9.8 |
| Operating engineers | 4,997 | 1,646 | 32.9 | 143 | 23 | 16.1 |
| Ironworkers | 95 | 8 | 8.4 | 35 | 3 | 8.6 |
| Painters | 5,381 | 1,362 | 25.3 | 205 | 57 | 27.8 |
| Pipefitters | 8,261 | 1,403 | 17.0 | 403 | 35 | 8.7 |
| Pipe and Steamfitters | 916 | 312 | 34.1 | 14 | 1 | 7.1 |
| Plasterers | 1,171 | 472 | 40.3 | 15 | 6 | 40.0 |
| Plumbers | 10,588 | 1,931 | 18.2 | 4,913 | 353 | 7.2 |
| Roofers | 4,184 | 1,328 | 31.7 | 228 | 41 | 18.0 |
| Sheetmetal | 6,707 | 1,363 | 20.3 | 1,125 | 122 | 10.8 |
| Sprinklerfitters | 1,761 | 214 | 12.2 | 183 | 5 | 2.7 |
| Structural Steel | 6,576 | 1,353 | 20.6 | 62 | 19 | 30.6 |
| Drywall tapers | 1,206 | 250 | 20.7 | 147 | 54 | 36.7 |
| Linemen (light and power) | 1,624 | 156 | 9.6 | 114 | 17 | 14.9 |
| Total | 118,419 | 25,067 | 21.2 | 19,065 | 2,180 | 11.4 |

Source: Bureau of Apprenticeship and Training, U.S. Department of Labor. Unpublished data tabulated for this study.

Note: Joint and nonjoint programs refer to union and open-shop programs, respectively.

the highest levels of minority participation were in occupations such as cement masons, painters and roofers, while relatively lower proportions were minorities in trades such as plumbing, carpentry, and sheetmetal work.

A high percentage of minorities as apprentices does not guarantee, of course, that minorities will come to be a large percentage of journeymen in a trade. The drop-out and cancellation rates are quite high. While the GAO critique of federal efforts notes the failure of many union and government programs to place minority apprentices in full-time work, it again fails to compare these results to the open-shop programs. But cancellation rates of apprentices calculated from the available data show that these are as high—if not substantially higher—in open-shop as in union programs (see table 4-9).

In sum, without extensive new analyses of the problems of minority recruitment and training in construction, it appears that whatever difficulties exist are common to both union and open-shop sectors of the industry and cannot be attributed to the influence of building trades unions alone.

**Table 4-9**
**Cancellation Rate in Union and Open-Shop Apprentice Programs, Selected Trades, 1976**
*(percent)*

| Trade | Joint (union) | Nonjoint (open shop) |
|---|---|---|
| Bricklayers | 19 | 67 |
| Cement masons | 24 | 42 |
| Electricians | 6 | 36 |
| Carpenters | 26 | 45 |
| Plumbers | 8 | 29 |
| Sheetmetal | 9 | 42 |

Source: Bureau of Apprenticeship and Training, U.S. Department of Labor. Unpublished data tabulated for this study.

Note: The cancellation rate is the total number of apprentices canceled during the year as a percent of total apprentices in a program at the beginning of 1976.

*Issues in Construction Training*

The contractor interview results, supplemented by discussions with a wide variety of other individuals, firms, and institutions involved in training in the industry, manifested a general dissatisfaction with the present state of apprenticeship and training in construction. Current concern, although by no means new, is focused around three interrelated issues:

1. The drop-out rate in many formal apprentice programs is very high.
2. Apprentice programs, especially in the basic trades, are perceived as being too long and as having too extensive a curriculum for increasingly specialized journeymen.
3. There is great interest in, but very little knowledge of, such innovations as incentive-based or performance apprenticeship programs with no fixed time spans, or new methods of training (such as "task training" used in some large open-shop construction firms).

All these issues are related to one basic problem: the distribution of the costs of worker training in construction. Formal apprenticeship programs divide the costs between workers (in lower earnings while apprentices and in foregone leisure while in class); employers, who make various types of contributions in both union and open-shop programs; and the government, which pays for classroom training as a part of vocational education. But in many trades a considerable proportion of the journeymen have progressed to that level without any formal apprenticeship.[13] The possibility of such informal training clearly can reduce the incentive of a worker to accede to the costs of formal apprenticeship. This economic disincentive is particularly true among open-shop workers who, although they may expect a lower wage on average than union journeymen, are required to invest the same number of years and hours if engaged in formal training in certified programs. Also, in many occupations, the curriculum is apparently outdated and the time span is too long for journeymen in either union or open-shop firms who will eventually specialize in only one or two aspects of the trade.[14] Contractors face a similar disincentive: they may lose money employing new apprentices (particularly if they start in certified programs at 50 percent of a union journeyman's rate) while they make money employing fourth-year apprentices who are fully productive while earning only 90 percent of a journeyman's hourly wage. Firms which cannot maintain a permanent work force have only an immediate incentive to hire older apprentices and to shun the startup costs of training new workers. This creates obvious problems in placing first-year apprentices; a problem which could be solved by lowering the initial wage.

Despite these difficulties, apprenticeship as a system of training is not wholly an anachronism or solely a mechanism to restrict entry into craft unions. Eighty-eight percent of union contractors and 75 percent of non-union commercial firms responded that some type of formal apprentice training was needed for most trades. But most of these firms reported that there were major institutional rigidities in the design and management of apprenticeship programs which hindered their responsiveness to the needs of some firms or to changing skills and technology. For this reason, all firms tended to supplement apprenticeship with various types of informal training in specialized skills peculiar to the firm and its products (see table 4-10). The extra cost of this training created some tension between adherence to the formal and general apprenticeship curriculum and the firm's immediate needs for skill development and productivity. While the basic rationale for formal apprenticeship is to impress upon firms the need for general training for some workers, an increasing misfit between formal training curricula and actual need will only cause more firms, as well as workers, to drop out of apprenticeship programs. Another response in the union sector to deficiencies in apprenticeship has focused on introducing performance rather than time standards for measuring advancement.[15] Traditional apprenticeship programs often specify a fixed number of hours which must be spent in class, in learning each skill on-site, and in each grade (that is, year) of training. Revisions of these programs have stressed pretraining of workers to establish whether the skill is known, short training modules if it is not, and immediate performance tests afterward. Workers can then progress individually and at their own pace rather than following the lockstep of a time-based program or—as often occurs—informally avoiding it altogether. Since these methods match the investment in training to the capabilities of each worker, they may help reduce the attrition of those who want and deserve rapid progression.

**Table 4-10**
**Union and Open-Shop Apprenticeship and Training**
*(percent)*

Apprentices
Do You Need Apprentice Programs?

| | All Union Companies | Nonunion Residential | Nonunion Commercial | Nonunion Heavy |
|---|---|---|---|---|
| Yes, for all trades | 76.7 | 38.9 | 46.9 | 15.8 |
| Yes, for some trades | 11.6 | 24.1 | 28.1 | 47.4 |
| No | 11.6 | 37.0 | 25.0 | 36.8 |

Do You Have Nonapprentice Training?

| | Union | Nonunion |
|---|---|---|
| Yes | 45.3 | 86.4 |
| No | 54.7 | 13.6 |

If Yes, What Type?

| | Union | Nonunion |
|---|---|---|
| On-the-job training | 74.4 | 97.8 |
| Informal training after hours | 10.3 | 18.0 |
| Short courses | 51.3 | 16.9 |

Source: 1976 survey by the Department of Housing and Urban Development and the Massachusetts Institute of Technology.
Note: 98.8 percent of the union companies had apprentice programs. 97.6 of those were certified.

Large open-shop firms, such as Brown and Root, and Daniels (now a subsidiary of Fluor) have also pioneered in creating new approaches to construction training. One of these, called task training, is the major open-shop alternative to formal apprenticeship. By subdividing construction skills into a series of individual tasks, it permits builders to train an unskilled local labor force on the site of a major construction project. Task training also permits the mixing of individual skills, called cross-training, into new occupations as the needs of a particular building or phase of construction dictate. This form of training is particularly suited to long-term projects in rural areas where its costs can be absorbed by the user or the local government as part of the project overhead or as a contribution to local economic development. While the training does not necessarily lead to journeyman status, many employees of these large firms progress rapidly through the various tasks within an occupation and are gradually promoted, on recommendation of their foreman or supervisor, to higher grades. These firms also keep records of which employees have been trained in various areas in which they build and use this information both for recruitment and labor needs planning in subsequent projects.

Recently, the Associated Builders and Contractors (ABC) has attempted to diffuse this approach to training throughout its membership. But with the exception of the Houston area—where several major construction users are helping to finance task training on their projects—most of the ABC's member firms are too small to support individually the level of training effort required. Also, the very diversity of open-shop firms, as well as the free-rider problem, make it difficult to maintain interest in or contributions to some formal training programs. (While this is also true among union firms, they are usually contractually obliged to contribute a certain number of cents per hour to apprenticeship programs.) As a result, ABC is investigating ways of centralizing task training in its local chapter headquarters for use by a number of firms. Where this has occurred, as it also has in Houston, a training fund is established by payments from larger firms and some users and then is drawn down as many companies, large and small, use different task training classes for their workers. This pooling of funds by large users and construction firms, coordinated by the Houston ABC and the local Business Roundtable in order to create a pool of qualified workers mainly for refinery and petrochemical work, has been attacked by the Houston and Gulf Coast Building Trades Council as a conspiracy to fix prices and drive out firms that use union labor and has been the subject of a 1979 antitrust suit. Whatever the validity of these charges, it is clear that the costs of developing and managing a task training system require the economies of scale of one large firm or the united efforts of many smaller firms working through an employer association. It is notable that this type of "collusion" is legal and encouraged in union apprenticeship programs where it is managed with the participation of worker represen- tatives, while it is both difficult to achieve and open to antitrust attacks in nonunion firms seeking to achieve comparable ends. An alternative here is to have workers pay more for their own training, rather than have construc- tion firms and users struggle either to allocate these costs between them or cooperate in passing them on to consumers.

In sum, with some substantial changes in curricula and format, formal apprenticeship programs are likely to continue to be useful for many medium-sized construction firms. This is particularly true if the government begins to certify programs which are more responsive to current training needs of union and open-shop firms and if employer associations and unions continue to make efforts to update training methods. However, smaller firms in both sectors will continue to rely largely on informal train- ing; very large contractors may continue to adopt task training approaches, particularly on large projects in competitive contexts which permit extra ex- penditures for training of what may be only temporary workers. The most substantial differences in the training approaches of union and open-shop firms appear to center on the specificity and relative informality of training in open-shop firms in contrast to the formal and general training, under joint supervision, in the union sector. However, with the exception of worker-union participation in training administration, there are more similarities than differences between union and open-shop firms over the basic issues of training cost and effectiveness: in both sectors, most firms are interested only in specific training with immediate impacts on produc- tivity. General training of broadly skilled journeymen ordinarily occurs only where it is imposed through formal union or government programs.

## Notes

1. Burke, "A Time of Reckoning for the Building Unions."

2. Haber and Levinson, *Labor Relations and Productivity in the Building Trades*, p. 189.

3. During the period 1949-1971, Lipsky and Farber found that while jurisdictional work stoppages increased in both absolute numbers and in relation to total worker-days, they tended to become shorter in duration. See David B. Lipsky and Henry S. Farber, "The Composition of Strike Ac- tivity in the Construction Industry," pp. 388-404.

4. U.S. Department of Labor, Labor Management Services Ad- ministration, *Exclusive Union Work Referral Systems in the Building Trades*, p. 25.

5. In one state, Massachusetts, the carpenters have attempted to solve this problem by signing a statewide agreement with specialty subcontractors

permitting them to employ some workers anywhere in the state for short periods of time. In other areas and for other trades, for example, the operating engineers in California and Nevada, the geographic area covered by locals is so large that these problems do not arise.

6. For example, the Merit Shop Construction Employment Agency at the offices of the Associated Builders and Contractors of Greater Houston, 1979.

7. The BLS does not usually report total on-site labor costs for these projects, so no strong conclusions can be drawn from these studies as to changes in labor productivity. But Rosefielde and Mills report new estimates of high rates of change in labor productivity, though negative increases in capital productivity, both due perhaps in part to the rapid rate of technological change in the industry. See Olsen, "Labor and Material Requirements for New School Construction," pp. 38-41, for an example of the BLS findings; and Rosefielde and Mills, "Is the Construction Industry Technologically Stagnant?" On the increased capital-intensity of building activity, particularly in highway construction, see J. Rossow and F. Moavenzadeh, "Productivity and Technology Change in Construction."

8. Quote from "The Butler Fact Sheet," Butler Manufacturing Company, 1978. Reprinted with permission.

9. See, for example, Richard L. Rowan and Lester Rubin, *Opening the Skilled Construction Trades to Blacks: A Study of the Washington and Philadelphia Plans for Minority Employment.* The Wharton School, University of Pennsylvania Press, 1972.

10. General Accounting Office, *Federal Efforts to Increase Minority Opportunities in Skilled Construction Craft Unions Have Had Little Success* (Washington, D.C., 1979).

11. Northrup and Foster, *Open Shop Construction*, p. 346.

12. The data is tabulated by the State and National Apprenticeship System (SNAPs) in the Bureau of Apprenticeship and Training (U.S. Department of Labor) but is unpublished.

13. The importance of formal training in achieving journeyman status differs considerably by trade. See Ray Marshall et al., *Training and Entry Into Union Construction.*

14. On the length of apprenticeship programs, Franklin holds an opposite view. See Franklin, "Are Construction Apprenticeships Too Long?"

15. The program in commercial carpentry developed by the Associated General Contractors is one example of this. See Dichl and Penner, *Commercial Carpentry.*

# Appendix 4A
# Article in the
# *Engineering News-Record*
# July 5, 1979

**Flexibility a Key in Work Awards**

The National Labor Relations Board has relied on economy and efficiency in rejecting ironworker claims to disputed work in two instances.

Use of multiskilled employees . . . produces a more efficient use of labor and reduced labor cost because these employees can shift from one task to another as the job requires and thereby put in a full day's work,'' the board explained in one of the cases.

The dispute arose during construction of a mausoleum at a Paterson, N.J., cemetery. The contractor, headquartered in Norcross, Ga., did the work with its nonunion employees. Local 483 of the ironworkers demanded the ironwork and picketed the cemetery to get it.

In awarding the work to the nonunion workers, the board noted that ''the construction of a mausoleum generally requires two hours of carpentry work, two hours of ironwork and/or two hours of cement work per day.'' The ironwork, it explained, basically involves placing and tying steel in the foundations, footings, crypt floor, walls and roof, and keeping the steel positioned properly as the concrete is poured. Because the ironworkers can do only this work, the board said, they would remain idle a good portion of the day, whereas the nonunion workers with their multiple skills can shift about as needed and put in a full day's work. Other factors that might have favored ironworkers were not present.

In the other case, Local 12 of the ironworkers claimed work a general contractor had assigned to laborers during construction of a parking garage in Pittsfield, Mass. The work involved unloading, handling, placing and fitting reinforcing wire mesh in preparation for pouring concrete for foundations, sidewalks and ramps. The contractor had a labor contract with laborers, none with ironworks.

The board found that neither area practice nor relative skills favored either union and relied on economy and efficiency to justify its award to laborers. The laborers ''are present on the jobsite and are able to perform other work at the site'' as well, it said.

Source: *Engineering News-Record*, July 5, 1979, p. 61. Reprinted with permission. © McGraw-Hill, Inc. All rights reserved.

# 5

# Relative Costs of Union and Open-Shop Construction

There is no simple way of reducing the findings on the union and open-shop wage and benefit differentials and on comparative work practices to concrete comparisons of construction costs. Moreover, no direct cost estimates or comparisons were made under the scope of the wage survey and contractor interviews. Although the open shop has now proved itself in many sectors of the marketplace (most always the best test of cost and efficiency) it is important to determine exactly the extent to which this success is due directly to lower hourly compensation costs in contrast to different skill mixes, the lack of union restrictions, disputes, and the like. Most cost comparisons of union and open-shop construction assume that the hourly wage and benefit differentials are the most significant element. The 1979 studies by the General Accounting Office on the Davis-Bacon Act, for example, compare average hourly wage rates between union and open-shop construction and conclude that since they differ significantly, nonunion construction is obviously less expensive than the union alternative. This approach to construction cost estimation is misguided, however. It focuses entirely on average wage differentials, without any allowance for offsetting skills and productivity, and ignores many other important components of total labor costs.

Unfortunately, there are very few rigorous studies which assess the relative costs of union and open-shop firms undertaking similar construction work at the same time and location. The reason is clear: such research is an expensive process, requiring the collection of large amounts of detailed data, and the exercising of considerable judgment as to what constitute common units of output. Although one way around this difficulty is to accept and compare bids from both union and open-shop firms for identical projects, even this approach is troublesome. First, the bid price, even if lump sum, is often not the final cost of construction. Change orders, extra work orders and claims may result in a very different—and almost always higher—final cost. Second, any delays in construction completion will result in higher costs and lost revenue or use to the buyer. Third, quality shortfalls may necessitate costly rework or result in higher maintenance costs. While construction users and general contractors have to compare bids in awarding work, they make these comparisons in a context rich with detail on a bidder's reputation for quality and performance. Indeed, users may be so satisfied with the performance of their usual contractors, that very few bids will be solicited. One study of the use of subcontractors by residential developers and builders reports that

> builders rarely seek competitive bids for new jobs. If they do so at all, they negotiate informally with one, sometimes a few subcontractors. Every so often builders obtain formal competitive bids, but only to verify market prices and to keep subcontractors competitive. Most builders prefer to stay with a few favorite subcontractors instead of simply shopping for the lowest price. This they do out of their concern for quality and dependability in adhering to construction schedules and responding to customer problems.[1]

Thus, simple comparison of a few bids in order to estimate the relative costs of union and open-shop construction is not useful without considerable ancillary information.

Again, the best approach to labor cost comparisons is to report them in the context of total final costs of virtually identical construction projects. While there are no examples of this type of research in the academic literature, an old but unique study by Mandelstamm (1965) of residential builders comes closest. Mandelstamm compared a large sample of bids from both union and open-shop builders in two cities. He also collected, through interviews, estimates of the impact of union work practices on construction efficiency. Mandelstamm's quantitative data shows that it is possible for skill and productivity of union workers to offset their higher wages. Table 5-1 presents his findings on median worker-hours per trade for identical single-family houses. Despite union-nonunion wage differentials which, on average, were roughly 23 percent, the total union wage bill (wage multiplied by hours worked) was only 11 percent higher in his comparisons. In almost all cases, the direct labor hours of the union trades were reported as substantially less than those of the nonunion workers. For at least four of the union crafts, this reduction in worker-hours offset almost entirely their higher wage per hour. Mandelstamm also concluded that none of the union work rules or other practices had a significant detrimental effect on productivity. He also found, as shown in table 5-1, that because of higher material costs and higher allowances for overhead and profit, the final cost estimate or price of nonunion housing was higher than that of the union firms.

While these findings are no longer relevant to any current estimation of the relative costs of union construction, they do illustrate that construction cost comparisons should not be made on the basis of wage rates alone. Also, Mandelstamm's findings foreshadow results in recent research on the effects of unions on productivity and costs. Recently, Freeman and Medoff (1979) and Brown and Medoff (1978) have reported that higher union wages in several industries are (or have been in the past) offset by higher produc-

**Table 5-1**

**Effects of Unions on Efficiency: Comparative Hours and Costs in Residential Construction**
*(median dollars and hours)*

| Trade | Price | | Wage Bill[a] | | Material Cost | | Overhead and Profit | | Labor Hours | |
|---|---|---|---|---|---|---|---|---|---|---|
| | Union | Non-union | Union | Non-union | Union | Non-union | Union | Non-union | Union | Non-union |
| Plastering | 603 | 495 | 436 | 338 | 121 | 121 | 49 | 31 | 132 | 138 |
| Brick veneer | 1,350 | 1,453 | 583 | 530 | 645 | 703 | 123 | 243 | 189 | 204 |
| Foundation | 1,257 | 1,216 | 391 | 336 | 588 | 599 | 279 | 369 | 132 | 121 |
| Basement floor | 435 | 435 | 176 | 150 | 192 | 200 | 85 | 106 | 52 | 58 |
| Painting | 575 | 563 | 402 | 304 | 80 | 113 | 149 | 196 | 143 | 192 |
| Electrical | 437 | 431 | 127 | 136 | 223 | 222 | 87 | 72 | 33 | 38 |
| Plumbing | 1,000 | 950 | 167 | 138 | 500 | 475 | 291 | 347 | 46 | 44 |
| Excavation | 241 | 253 | 72 | 46 | — | — | 111 | 149 | 23 | 24 |
| Heating | 875 | 900 | 140 | 134 | 467 | 504 | 269 | 262 | 42 | 64 |
| Sheet metal | 91 | 123 | 26 | 40 | 22 | 50 | 43 | 35 | 8 | 20 |
| Glazing | 156 | 220 | 15 | NA | 115 | 157 | 27 | NA | 5 | 10 |
| Carpentry | 4,066[b] | 4,833[b] | 1,186 | 1,187 | 2,880 | 3,496 | 0[b] | 0[b] | 288 | 438 |
| Roofing | 324 | 360 | 72 | 62 | 162 | 132 | 90 | 91 | 16 | 26 |
| Totals | 11,409[b] | 12,231[b] | 3,776[c] | 3,401[c] | 5,994 | 6,772 | 1,574[bc] | 1,900[bc] | 1,107 | 1,377 |

Source: Allan B. Mandelstamm, "The Effect of Unions on Efficiency in the Residential Construction Industry: A Case Study," *Industrial and Labor Relations Review* 18(1965):507. Reprinted with permission.

Note: NA means not available. This table includes only those trades in which medians were available for both union and nonunion contractors in Bay City. Thus, tile-setting and floor finishing have been excluded because only union men participated. Sewer installation has also been excluded: no estimates were recorded on a contractor-to-contractor basis for this trade. Numbers have been rounded. A few contractors employed both union and nonunion workmen. In determining the median for this table, such contractors have been excluded.

[a] All figures for wage bill include contractor estimates for fringe benefits and labor-connected insurance.

[b] The price for carpentry is exclusive of the overhead and profit of the contractor performing this function. The totals for price and overhead and profit reflect this omission.

[c] The totals for wage bill and overhead and profits do not include glazing because no figures were available for nonunion contractors in this trade.

tivity of workers. And Clark (1979) has shown that the "shock effect" of unionization of cement plants has resulted in management reactions which raised productivity above levels which prevail in nonunion plants. Clark found that the combination of costlier labor and union grievance procedures required management to pay more attention to scheduling, equipment maintenance, and supervision, and that this attention resulted in higher productivity even in the absence of changes in worker skills or quality. None of this evidence, of course, proves that all union labor is necessarily as productive as nonunion workers; it just suggests that, contrary to conventional wisdom, it is at least possible for a high-wage union labor force to produce at unit costs comparable to lower-paid workers.

Following the methodology of Brown and Medoff, Allen (1979) used cross-section data from the 1972 census of construction industries to test for the impact of unions on productivity in construction. Controlling for capital employed, labor skill, and region, Allen finds that value-added per worker-hour is 29 percent greater in unionized construction firms. He also shows that if this extra productivity can be entirely attributable to labor, then union members are at least 38 percent more productive than other workers in construction. This extra productivity nearly offsets the union wage premium which Allen estimates at 43 percent. While there are numerous difficulties in making broad statistical estimates of this sort, the central problem is not to confuse union productivity effects with union cost or employer price effects. Any measure of value-added that is used to measure productivity necessarily compounds price and quality into one measure of output: dollar volume. If variations between firms in value-added per worker reflect variations in price rather than in quantity of output, then only a union cost effect is evident, not a productivity effect. Allen's research has to assume that construction product markets are so competitive that any major price differences between union and nonunion firms would have been eroded. But due to the substantial differences in degree of unionization of construction by product market and geographic area (reported in chapter 2) this assumption may not be valid. Indeed, when Allen experiments with greater price variations between regions as a causal factor (by constraining the coefficient on the area price index to be equal to one), the union productivity effect was substantially reduced—perhaps to around 20 percent. Nonetheless, this type of study does establish that there may very well be some significant relationship between unionization and productivity. Allen concludes, however, by saying it is not clear from his analysis exactly what the link is.

Speed (1978) has adopted an approach similar to Mandelstamm's in estimating the effects of unions on construction costs. He estimates labor costs on a union and open-shop basis for thirteen field crafts and two overhead occupations (field engineer and office staff) for a representative million-worker-hour industrial project in the southeastern United States.[2] His initial comparisons focus on eight categories of labor cost for a union project built without a project labor agreement and for the same project built open-shop at "open-shop rates." He assumes hourly wage differentials of, on average, 21 percent—roughly comparable to those found in similar areas in the 1976 survey—and substantial differences in hourly benefits (see table 5-2).

The differences in the total wage bill are in this case, however, greater than those due to the observed differentials in compensation. This is because Speed adds his estimates of the extra savings which can accrue to the open-shop contractor by using helpers and by avoiding unproductive expenditures on union stewards (assumed to be only 60 percent productive), potential disputes, or mandatory work breaks (see table 5-3, columns 2 and 3). In terms of percentages, the savings for the open-shop contractor in direct labor (due to lower wages, skill mix, and helpers) and in benefits comprise roughly half of the total labor cost differential.

Speed also estimates the cost of this same project under different conditions: where, due to labor market pressures, the open-shop contractor has to pay close to union rates to obtain labor, and where the union contractor operates under a project agreement. In these circumstances, as shown in table 5-3, columns 1 and 4, the total labor cost differentials virtually disappear. In particular, the use of helpers or a subjourneyman wage rate, permissible under many current project agreements, provides significant economies to the union firm, as does the reduction in the (assumed) costs of disputes due to a no-strike clause.[3] The open-shop firm still bears the slightly higher cost of extra supervision, and to this is added the substantially greater expenditures on direct labor due to higher wage rates. Under these circumstances, which are not unusual in many areas of the country, the total union-open-shop labor cost difference comes to only 3 percent. Of course, proponents of open-shop construction prefer to make the first comparison.

In sum, while neither the research findings of Mandelstamm and Allen nor the cost estimates of Speed are conclusive, since any of their individual assumptions or findings on costs may be questioned, they do indicate most of the necessary elements involved in making valid cost comparisons. Yet it is clear that the cost differential between union and open-shop firms is not constant but depends on a variety of factors, including the type of construction, the state of the labor and product markets, and the particular terms of the union contract in effect.

**Table 5-2**
**Direct Wage and Benefit-Cost Comparison for Union and Open-Shop Industrial Construction**

| Craft Description | Craft Mix (Percent) | Worker Hours per Craft | Journeyman Rate per Hour | Direct Labor Cost | Fringe Benefit Rate per Hour | Benefit Cost | Total Labor Cost |
|---|---|---|---|---|---|---|---|
| | | | **Closed-Shop Contruction Cost** | | | | |
| Office force | 2.43 | 24,300 | 5.00 | 121,500 | | | 121,500 |
| Field engineers | 2.41 | 24,100 | 8.00 | 192,800 | | | 192,800 |
| Laborers | 23.27 | 232,700 | 6.00 | 1,396,200 | .95 | 221,065 | 1,617,265 |
| Carpenters | 8.73 | 87,300 | 9.32 | 813,636 | .95 | 82,935 | 896,571 |
| Millwrights | 5.02 | 50,200 | 9.87 | 495,474 | .95 | 47,690 | 543,164 |
| Brick masons | .58 | 5,800 | 9.46 | 54,868 | 1.76 | 10,208 | 65,076 |
| Iron workers | 9.64 | 96,400 | 9.73 | 937,972 | .95 | 91,580 | 1,029,552 |
| Cement finishers | 1.34 | 13,400 | 9.82 | 131,588 | .95 | 12,730 | 144,318 |
| Operators | 5.03 | 50,300 | 9.77 | 491,431 | .95 | 47,785 | 539,216 |
| Sheetmetal | .02 | 200 | 10.55 | 2,110 | 1.89 | 378 | 2,488 |
| Teamsters | 2.25 | 22,500 | 7.39 | 166,275 | .95 | 21,375 | 187,650 |
| Boilermakers | 5.49 | 54,900 | 9.50 | 521,550 | 2.67 | 146,583 | 668,133 |
| Pipefitters | 20.50 | 205,000 | 11.10 | 2,275,500 | 1.43 | 293,150 | 2,568,650 |
| Painters | .04 | 400 | 10.03 | 4,010 | 1.16 | 464 | 4,474 |
| Electricians | 13.25 | 132,500 | 9.35 | 1,238,875 | 1.04 | 137,800 | 1,376,675 |
| Total | 100.00 | 1,000,000 | 8.84 | 8,843,789 | 1.11 | 1,113,743 | 9,957,532 |

## Open-Shop Construction Cost

| | | | | | | |
|---|---|---|---|---|---|---|
| Office force | 3.84 | 38,400 | 4.50 | 172,800 | .15 | 5,760 | 178,560 |
| Field engineers | 3.25 | 32,500 | 7.00 | 227,500 | .15 | 4,875 | 232,375 |
| Laborers | 14.32 | 143,200 | 4.30 | 615,760 | .15 | 21,480 | 637,240 |
| Carpenters | 12.75 | 127,500 | 7.45 | 949,875 | .15 | 19,125 | 969,000 |
| Millwrights | 8.81 | 88,100 | 8.30 | 731,230 | .15 | 13,215 | 744,445 |
| Brick masons | .82 | 8,200 | 8.30 | 68,060 | .15 | 1,230 | 69,290 |
| Iron workers | 10.42 | 104,200 | 8.30 | 864,860 | .15 | 15,630 | 880,490 |
| Cement finishers | 1.49 | 14,900 | 7.45 | 111,005 | .15 | 2,235 | 113,240 |
| Operator engineers | 4.16 | 41,600 | 8.30 | 345,280 | .15 | 6,240 | 351,520 |
| Sheetmetal | .02 | 200 | 8.30 | 1,660 | .15 | 30 | 1,690 |
| Boilermakers | 2.51 | 25,100 | 8.30 | 208,330 | .15 | 3,765 | 212,095 |
| Pipefitters | 25.27 | 252,700 | 8.30 | 2,097,410 | .15 | 37,905 | 2,135,315 |
| Painters | 1.00 | 10,000 | 7.40 | 74,000 | .15 | 1,500 | 75,500 |
| Electricians | 9.95 | 99,500 | 8.30 | 825,850 | .15 | 14,925 | 840,775 |
| Truck drivers | 1.39 | 13,900 | 6.55 | 91,045 | .15 | 2,085 | 93,130 |
| Total | 100.00 | 1,000,000 | 7.38 | 7,384,665 | .15 | 150,000 | 7,534,665 |

Source: Speed, William S., "Construction Labor Cost Comparison of Open and Closed Shop Construction Projects," *American Association of Cost Engineers Transactions*, 1978, pp. 141, 142. © 1978 by the American Association of Cost Engineers. Reprinted with permission.

**Table 5-3**
**Total Labor-Cost Comparison for Union and Open-Shop Industrial Construction**
*(dollars)*

| | *(1)* Union-Shop Project with Project Labor Agreement | *(2)* Union-Shop Project without Project Labor Agreement | *(3)* Open Shop with Open-Shop Rates | *(4)* Open Shop with Union Rates and 40¢/hr. Benefits |
|---|---|---|---|---|
| Direct costs | 8,843,789 | 8,843,789 | 7,384,665 | 9,192,111 |
| Benefits | +953,493 | +1,113,743 | +150,000 | +371,640 |
| Stewards | +65,458 | +87,277 | — | — |
| Helpers | −539,471 | — | −420,926 | −523,950 |
| Strikes and jurisdictional disputes | — | +221,094 | — | — |
| Check in and out breaks | 518,395 | +1,139,275 | 392,313 | 498,076 |
| Tools and material warehousing | — | 96,016 | — | — |
| Added supervision | — | — | +53,063 | +53,063 |
| Totals | 9,841,664 | 11,501,194 | 7,559,115 | 9,590,940 |
| Cost per worker hour | 9.84 | 11.50 | 7.55 | 9.59 |

Source: Speed, William S., "Construction Labor Cost Comparison of Open and Closed Shop Construction Projects," *American Association of Cost Engineers Transactions*, 1978, p. 150. © 1978 by the American Association of Cost Engineers. Reprinted with permission.

**Notes**

1. "Subcontractors and Homebuilders," in Harvard-MIT Joint Center for Urban Studies, *Research Report*, April 1979, p. 2. Reprinted with permission.

2. William S. Speed, "Construction Labor Cost Comparison." Mr. Speed is a certified construction cost engineer who has worked for both BE & K and Rust Engineering, open-shop and union construction firms respectively. The firms operate largely in the Southeast.

3. For the terms of the project agreement, Speed uses clauses similar to those found in the National Constructors Association Industrial Agreement.

# 6 The Impact of the Davis-Bacon Act

The Davis-Bacon Act, one of the first articles of federal labor legislation, was enacted in 1931 to protect local workers in federally financed construction projects from the competition of lower-paid, nonlocal labor. While the intense competition for public construction work during the Depression provided impetus for its passage, several similar bills had been introduced in Congress at various times during the more prosperous years of the 1920s. Although equivalent laws were passed at the state level before 1931, these were apparently motivated by causes more related to previous labor legislation shortening work hours than to disruptive labor market conditions. What brought final legislative success in Congress was a convergence of economic pressures due to the Depression, which motivated a broad coalition to support the bill. The building trades were fearful of the erosion of their wage standards due to high unemployment; local contractors were against "cutthroat" competition by itinerant workers and firms; and some politicians fought the disruption of employment in their localities by imported workers particularly, as one Congressman put it, by "cheap colored labor . . . that is in competition with white labor throughout the country."[1]

Despite these convoluted origins, the basic act itself is quite simple. It authorizes that "specifications for every contract . . . shall contain a provision stating the minimum wages to be paid various classes of laborers and mechanics which shall be based upon the wages that will be determined by the Secretary of Labor to be prevailing for the corresponding classes of laborers and mechanics employed on projects of a character similar to the contract work in the city, town . . . or other civil subdivision . . . in which the work is to be performed . . . " Much of the subsequent controversy over the act has focused on the administrative interpretation of such terms as "prevailing rate of wages" or "work of a similar nature," because these have been seen as part of the Department of Labor's predilection for determining the union rate as the prevailing wage. Critics like Thieblot (1975), Gould (1971), Gujarati (1967) have contended that the department, in misusing the considerable discretion given it by the act, has frequently established rates of pay which do not reflect "the prevailing rate of wages" in an area and thus result in inflated construction costs. For example, the department defines prevailing wages, under one of three rules, as either:

1.  The rate of wages paid in the area in which the work is to be performed, to the *majority* of those employed in that classification in construction in the area similar to the proposed undertaking; or
2.  In the event that there is not a majority paid at the same rate, then the rate paid to the greatest number: Provided, such greater number constitutes *30 percent* of those employed; or
3.  In the event that less than 30 percent of those so employed receive the same rate, then the average rate.[2]

These rules, particularly the emphasis on either the "majority" or "30 percent" being paid "at the same rate," have been seen to unduly favor determinations of union rates as prevailing because of their contractual uniformity by trade and area. Other recurrent criticisms of the administration of the act include the conditions under which the department either undertakes, or should undertake, a wage survey to determine local prevailing rates; the appropriate classifications for occupation, areas, and types of construction work; and the right to appeal determinations. Poor or biased administration of the act has been said to ". . . force nonunion employers (if they want to participate in government projects) to pay higher wage rates than otherwise would be required to attract competent crews, and in turn, this effectively denies the government the savings associated with open shop construction."[3]

Both the administration of the act and its alleged impact on construction costs are subject to empirical study and verification. Behind those issues, however, lies a larger question of the basic purpose or rationale for the act. While congressional intent is always subject to debate, it appears that the initial purpose of the act was solely to respond to the anarchic conditions in construction labor markets caused by the Depression. Yet the nature of this response, even if justified by the exigencies of the moment, set up a continuing system of administered wages which some immediately recognized as antithetical to the principles of competitive markets. For example, in 1931 the U.S. Comptroller General testified that:

> however desirable the contrary may be, it seems clear that in the present state of law the proposal to fix by contract the minimum rate of wages the contractor must pay his employees in the doing of the contract work . . . clashes with the long recognized intent and purpose of section 3709, Revised Statutes, in that it removes from competitive bidding on the project an important element of cost and tends to defeat the purpose of the statute—that is, to obtain a need of the United States, authorized by law to be acquired, at a cost no greater than the amount of the bid of the low responsible bidder, after full and free competitive bidding.[4]

Many recent attacks on Davis-Bacon, as well as on other articles of labor legislation such as the minimum wage, continue to reflect this basic belief in "full and free competitive bidding" and to reject regulatory mechanisms which fix wages or prices. For example, prominent macroeconomists ranging from the conservative Allan Greenspan, to the liberal Walter Heller, have argued that "a government that is dead serious about fighting inflation ought to put an end to the laws that make government an accomplice in cost and price-propping actions . . . such as the Davis-Bacon Act."[5]

Current criticisms of the act, typified by the 1979 General Accounting Office (GAO) report, thus assert that, first, the act is outmoded, because the conditions under which it was passed no longer exist; second, the act is poorly administered and raises wages above those actually prevailing; and third, both the higher wages and the resulting higher construction costs are inflationary. During 1979 legislators at both the state and federal level made several attempts to repeal or amend Davis-Bacon. Buoyed by a strong conservative caucus in both houses of Congress and in states such as Alabama, Florida, Texas, and Utah—as well as by a general climate supportive of deregulation and antiinflation measures—their efforts gathered more attention and votes than had previous repeal measures.

In sum, the impact of the Davis-Bacon Act on the level of wages and on the cost of federal construction has been a source of controversy for many years. Yet, because the nature of the debate has been more polemical than substantive, there is no conclusive evidence on the overall impact that Davis-Bacon has had. Most previous studies consist only of examples and illustrations of particular wage determinations which will raise the wage level (and perhaps the final cost) of selected projects. But since over fifteen thousand project and area wage determinations are made every year, it is not clear whether a few examples or even a small sample are representative of the whole.

The wage data and contractor interviews generated by the 1976 survey provide an opportunity to study the impact of Davis-Bacon determinations on a fairly widespread and consistent basis. The wage survey permits a unique comparison of union, open-shop and Davis-Bacon rates by type of construction in eight metropolitan areas. The interview data also provide insights from open-shop contractors as to the possible efficiency impacts of such prevailing wage laws. These findings can be combined with others to provide a more comprehensive analysis of the economic impact of the act. In addition, attention has to be paid to the original intent of the legislation, subsequently reaffirmed by Congress, which was in part to establish the principle that wages should not be an element in the competition for government contracts. While antithetical to economists' and others' belief in the value of competitive markets, this principle is central to the philosophy of trade unionism and, indeed, to most of the existing legislation on labor standards. Thus, debates over the cost impact of the act quickly become entangled in more philosophical arguments over the proper role of government in regulating labor markets.

**Market and Prevailing Wages**

One of the criticisms of the administration of the Davis-Bacon Act is that the Department of Labor establishes union rates as prevailing even when market or open-shop rates are prevalent in an area. The evidence from the 1976 wage survey does not completely sustain this. For categories of construction similar to commercial building, nearly all the Davis-Bacon rates are virtually identical to the union wage scales in each metropolitan area.[6] (See appendix B). Moreover, in metropolitan areas like Grand Rapids, Baltimore, Atlanta, and New Orleans, where there is a significant amount of open-shop commercial construction, this is not reflected in the prevailing wages. Since the open-shop wages in these areas are, on average, substantially lower than union rates, even the use of the average of the two as the Davis-Bacon determination would lower nominal labor costs. Yet, because of the dispersion of wage rates in the open-shop sector, reliance on the majority or the 30 percent rule does virtually guarantee that the union rate will become the prevailing wage even in relatively strong open-shop areas.

But for residential construction, the results of the wage comparison are much more varied. Three different patterns are evident in the eight areas:

1. The two areas with relatively low open-shop activity, Boston and Kansas City, have prevailing wages for residential work identical to union commercial building rates;
2. In two cities with moderate open-shop activity, the residential prevailing rates are higher than the open-shop average wages but significantly lower than the union commercial rates; and
3. In four cities with a large nonunion sector, the residential prevailing rates are *lower* than the average open-shop rate.

With this kind of diversity in results, it is difficult to generalize about the impact of Davis-Bacon on wages in residential construction. Clearly, the act and its administration do not tend to raise wages in this sector in some areas. On the other hand, in areas which are largely union, the union commerical building rate does tend to spread over all public construction—even when considerable residential work is apparently open-shop. So, without arguing the validity of each wage determination on the basis of the rules—or without challenging the rationale for the rules themselves—it is clear that the administrators of the act are more responsive to reporting open-shop wages than their critics admit. This observation is substantiated by the findings of two other studies. The 1979 GAO report, for example, found that on the basis of its sample of thirty localities, 34 percent of the wages established as "prevailing" were nonunion rates. And, an internal review by the Department of Housing and Urban Development of prevailing wages established for federal housing programs, found that 77 percent were open-shop rates. Significantly, even states with an apparent high proportion of union construction, such as New York and Ohio, had a majority of nonunion wages established as prevailing for residential construction (see table 6-1).

**Table 6-1**
**U.S. Department of Labor Wage Determinations for 3106 Areas and Projects, Residential Construction, by State, 1978**

| State | All-Union Wages Mandated | Nonunion Wages Mandated | Mixed Wages Mandated |
|-------|------------------------|------------------------|---------------------|
| Kansas | 10 | 94 | 1 |
| Alaska | 29 | | |
| Louisiana | 17 | 47 | |
| Illinois | 99 | 2 | 1 |
| New Hampshire | | 10 | |
| Maine | 1 | 13 | 2 |
| Vermont | | 14 | |
| Iowa | 4 | 92 | 3 |
| Kentucky | | 120 | |
| Georgia | | 159 | |
| Tennessee | | 95 | |
| Virginia | | 95 | |
| Florida | | 67 | |
| North Carolina | | 100 | |
| South Carolina | | 46 | |
| Puerto Rico | | 1 | |
| Virgin Islands | | 1 | |
| New York | 14 | 48 | |
| Pennsylvania | 18 | 21 | 28 |
| Texas | 31 | 223 | |
| Washington, D.C. | | | Mixed |
| Massachusetts | 14 | | |
| Connecticut | 3 | 3 | 2 |
| Indiana | 3 | 87 | 2 |
| Rhode Island | | | |
| Ohio | 11 | 77 | |
| Michigan | 39 | 17 | 27 |
| Arizona | 4 | 10 | |
| Hawaii | 4 | | |
| Idaho | 6 | 38 | |
| Nevada | 2 | 15 | |
| Utah | | 29 | |
| South Dakota | | 66 | 1 |
| North Dakota | | 42 | 11 |
| Washington | 6 | 28 | 5 |
| New Jersey | 5 | 16 | |
| Delaware | | 3 | |
| Wisconsin | 16 | 40 | 16 |
| West Virginia | 23 | 29 | 3 |
| Nebraska | 3 | 90 | |

**Table 6-1** *(continued)*

| State | All-Union Wages Mandated | Nonunion Wages Mandated | Mixed Wages Mandated |
|---|---|---|---|
| Maryland | | 24 | |
| Oregon | 6 | 27 | 3 |
| Missouri | 19 | 96 | |
| Oklahoma | | 77 | |
| Arkansas | | 75 | |
| New Mexico | 9 | 23 | |
| California | 43 | 8 | 7 |
| Montana | 48 | 4 | 4 |
| Colorado | | 31 | 32 |
| Minnesota | 34 | 29 | 24 |
| Wyoming | | 22 | 1 |
| American Samoa | | 1 | |
| Guam | | 1 | |
| Pacific Islands | | 1 | |
| Alabama | | 63 | 4 |
| Mississippi | | 82 | |
| Total number of areas or projects | 524 | 2404 | 178 |
| Percent of all determinations | 16.8 | 77.3 | 5.9 |

Source: Testimony of Secretary Patricia Harris, Department of Housing and Urban Development, before the Subcommittee on Housing and Urban Affairs of the Senate Committee on Banking, Housing, and Urban Affairs, May 2, 1979.

While the sample size of both the 1976 wage survey and the 1979 GAO report are too small to draw very significant conclusions about the overall administration of the act, the results do tend to discredit claims that its administration completely ignores nonunion wages. Given the number of wage determinations made every year, there is always ample opportunity for administrative bias and error. While the GAO report contains many examples of this, it is also clear that the current determinations now reflect significant attention to surveying and reporting open-shop wages when they are, in fact, prevailing in an area.

Nonetheless, the results of the wage survey and contractor interviews reported in chapters 3 and 4 indicate that any administrative definition of "prevailing" wages or occupations in construction is likely to be difficult to articulate and administer. Open-shop firms may not abide by the traditional occupational classification of union construction and wages may vary significantly even within subsectors of the major categories of construction, for example, between high-rise housing and residential rehabilitation. Indeed, any unbiased observer looking at the high degree of wage dispersion even within one occupation in an area would be hard put to define a "prevailing wage." As a consequence, if the administration of the act were to become even more responsive to truly prevailing wages and occupations in construction, it would undoubtedly become more complex and costly.

**Prevailing Wages and Construction Costs**

Although the general impact of the Davis-Bacon Act on wage levels is not clearly established, most studies nonetheless conclude that the act results in the determination of rates higher than those actually "prevailing." Studies such as the one by the Council on Wage and Price Stability (COWPS) then go on to assume that these higher wages result in proportionately higher total construction costs.[7] For example, if it can be shown that Department of Labor determinations are 20 percent higher than market (that is, open-shop) wages and labor constitutes roughly 20 percent of total building costs, as COWPS estimates, the effect of the act will be to raise public construction costs by 4 percent. This becomes an impressive statistic when the presumed 4 percent increase is multiplied by several billion dollars in annual federal construction outlays: COWPS concluded that changes in Davis-Bacon could save several hundred million dollars in federal building costs each year.

This approach to construction cost analysis is not correct, however. It is based on the implicit assumption that workers with different wage levels have equivalent productivity and thus can be seen as perfect substitutes in making cost comparisons. The only empirical work which tested this assumption, that by Mandelstamm, found that it was fallacious. Mandelstamm compared the total wage bill on union-built, single-family housing to that on similar housing constructed by nonunion contractors. While he found that union hourly rates were substantially higher than nonunion wages, the higher wages were partially offset by the greater productivity of union workers. As a result, the total wage bill was roughly equivalent on the two sets of housing. Thus, as noted in chapter 5, no conclusion as to the impact on construction costs can or should be drawn on the basis of wage comparisons alone.

The uncertain relation between wage levels and final construction costs has been overlooked by government analysts. Both Goldfarb and Morral, and the 1979 GAO report develop cost impacts of Davis-Bacon for all federal construction using the crude methodology described above: adjusting the wage bill by a percentage which they find reflects the wage differential imposed by Davis-Bacon.[8] For example, Goldfarb and Morral find that union wages in a sample of cities are 2.1 percent above average wages (combining union and open-shop wages) in commercial construction, and 5.4 percent in residential construction. They then conclude: "Since public construction in 1972 totaled about $30.2 billion and labor compensation is estimated to be about 35 percent of total costs, percentage savings of 2.1 to 5.4 percent translate into dollar savings of $222 million to $571 million for 1972." Clearly, if there are any union or labor productivity differentials at all which offset these higher wages, paying lower wages would only result in the added cost of extra worker-hours. Since the final wage bill as a component of building costs is the result of hourly wages multiplied by hours worked, the impact on total cost of reducing wages is indeterminate. Thus, higher union wages may not necessarily result in higher construction costs.

The results of the interviews with open-shop contractors also provide evidence that their response to higher prevailing wages in public work results in actions which limit the extent to which these are passed on in final costs. Several of the nonunion contractors interviewed pointed out that by offering higher wages on public projects they were able to attract workers with more training or experience. And over half of the nonunion contractors used the difference between wages on their public and private work to reward their most loyal and productive workers by selecting them to work on the public construction. This selection was also necessary to ensure productivity adequate to compete for public work. It was also clear from the interviews that open-shop contractors, when required to pay higher wages to their workers, devoted more attention not only to worker selection and training, but also to on-site project management such as scheduling and equipment maintenance. Since management actions alone can contribute enormously to the productivity of labor, intensive on-site management probably has an even greater impact on reducing project cost than the worker selection effects.

While these factors worked to offset the impact of higher wages, contractors also stressed that many aspects of the law tended to raise their costs. The most important of these was administrative inattention to open-shop occupations and skill levels. If, when nonunion wages are adopted as prevailing, union craft jurisdictions and skill levels are still used, contractors will be hindered by the act. Under these circumstances, contractors who normally cross-train men or who use an undifferentiated work crew have to report their workers under a particular union occupation. In fact, if the reporting rules are strictly followed, an open-shop contractor may have to pay a general building mechanic several different rates at different times depending on whether the worker is doing ironwork, carpentry, or masonry. This occurs most frequently on some aspects of housing and heavy construction.[9] Also, any absence of helper categories in the Davis-Bacon determinations provides a nonunion contractor with a choice between the lesser of two evils: he can pay his helpers the journeyman's wage, with obvious cost implications; or he can attempt to establish and enroll them in certified apprentice programs. Since these must be structured along craft union lines in order to be acceptable to the federal Bureau of Apprenticeship and Training or the State Apprenticeship Councils, the helper will often be trained at an inappropriate occupational breadth or skill level, given the normal operations of his employer. Contractors also found the requirement of weekly reporting of payrolls—to attest that they were indeed paying the determined wage—burdensome, but no quantitative estimates of these costs were obtained.

The net result of these potentially positive and negative impacts on the efficiency of open-shop contractors is not clear. If the congressional testimony of some contractors is typical, the net impact is substantially negative. One construction firm estimated that the combination of higher wages and benefits (plus indirect costs on these) and overhead costs due to reporting requirements raised the final construction costs on two federal housing projects by 11 percent in one instance and 62 percent in another.[10] Again, while there is no evidence that this example is typical, no current analyses or cost estimates are available which contradict it. Given the potentially enormous impact of Davis-Bacon and similar local laws on public construction, the government has been seriously remiss in not undertaking some representative and unbiased analyses of its direct effects on final construction costs.

**Spillover Effects and Inflation**

Critics of the Davis-Bacon Act also assert that the act operates to increase union market power and this results in both higher union wages in construction and the spillover of these high wages—or rapid rates of increase—into other sectors of the economy. But there is little or no evidence from the academic research literature that the act raises wages or costs on nonfederally assisted construction in local geographic areas. The wage spillover effect, if any, should occur primarily in open-shop firms which do some public work. The contractor interviews indicated that open-shop firms handle the wage discrepancy between private (nonunion) work and public construction at union rates in various ways. Most firms use two separate sets of crews which specialize in the two respective categories of work. Some firms rotate their workers through the higher-wage projects, while a few paid the higher wages for all work. Still other open-shop firms avoid public work completely. The diversity of policies by which open-shop firms react suggests that any direct wage spillover effect is confined apparently to a relatively few firms.

In addition, there is little or no evidence that construction wages spill over to other sectors and, through a demonstration effect, increase union or other wages in industry or services. Although there are patterns of wage relationships in the American economy, the small amount of empirical work done on these patterns has not established any strong link between construction and other sectors. Flanagan (1976) finds some correlation between construction wage increases and changes in the manufacturing wage level, but this may be interpreted as coincidental: both were increasing at roughly the same time. Bourdon (1979) in a study of pattern-following in collective bargaining, found that the leadership of major industrial unions paid virtually no attention to construction wage settlements even though collective bargaining gains by some industrial unions did spill over into other manufacturing sectors. Thus, even if the Davis-Bacon Act has some impact on the level or rate of increase of union wages in construction, it cannot be said to have a very strong effect on wages in other sectors of the economy.

### Conclusions: Costs and Benefits

The previous studies of the impact of Davis-Bacon on construction wages and, implicitly, on construction costs are usually one of two types. Those openly hostile to the act gather and present only examples of either (alleged) administrative error or cases of apparent substantial changes in construction cost due to a particular prevailing wage decision. More neutral observers, such as COWPS, attempt less biased and more comprehensive studies, but their conclusions are questionable due to the assumptions they make about the independence of wages and worker productivity. As noted above, some microeconomic equilibrating forces may tend to produce productivity increases to compensate, if increases in hourly wages are mandated by the act. However, nonwage impacts of the act on open-shop firms may tend to increase its cost impact beyond any increase in hourly wage costs. In sum, the key issue in any Davis-Bacon analysis is the extent to which increased productivity offsets the higher wages and the indirect costs which may arise due to prevailing wage determinations. While it may be obvious in some cases that it does not, this issue has never been systematically addressed. While the 1976 survey did not generate any detailed data on individual worker productivity, it did find that there were tremendous variations in skills and types of workers within and between the union and open-shop sectors. These findings preclude wholesale asumptions or allegations about relative union productivity. Thus the impact of Davis-Bacon on construction costs needs to be analyzed on the basis of an unbiased sample of the unit labor costs and final costs of particular construction projects, both union and open-shop, before any general conclusions can be drawn.

In lieu of any new research, however, the wage survey does show that there is no evidence of a "prevailing wage" in nonunion labor markets. Due to the dispersion of open-shop wages, almost any attempt to determine a prevailing wage will tend to favor the choice of the union rate, simply because it is uniformly set by contract. The use of an average rate, particularly where this can be identified for different sectors of construction, may be the best administrative compromise in markets where there is a combination of union and open-shop activity. Of course, the costs of sample surveys to determine a valid mean wage and the survey problems of reconciling occupational and skill definitions are substantial. This is particularly true in areas where open-shop activity is strong in some types of smaller-scale commercial and industrial construction. In fact, one of the major drawbacks to the present system of administering the act is that it often lumps all types of residential or commercial work together and just determines an area rate for each trade. Since there is considerable variety in residential work, for example, with different degrees of union or open-shop activity in each of the different types, these categories of construction are too broadly defined. Yet the reporting, surveying, and administrative costs could become substantial if an attempt were really made to respond to the complexities of determining prevailing wage levels in different submarkets within the construction industry.

The obvious alternative to changing the administration of the act is, as is continually suggested, to repeal it or reform it to the point of repeal. Those who believe that the act gives an uncompetitive advantage to the building trades unions and raises construction costs obviously favor repeal. Those who believe in more competitive, but not necessarily nonunion, labor markets may also feel that the government has no need to regulate construction wages and would also support repeal.[11] Certainly, the fact that most open-shop construction wages are, on the average, higher than local manufacturing wages vitiates any argument that wage regulation in construction is generally necessary or defensible on the grounds of equity or income distribution, as in the case of minimum wage laws. On the other hand, the fact that a considerable amount of public construction is now done by open-shop firms at least means that not only union workers benefit from the distributive effects of the law.

Finally, *if* the act is carefully administered and in fact determines rates which are actually prevailing, its independent impact on construction wages and costs is likely to be much smaller than its critics allege. It will then serve only to protect local workers and contractors from "outside" wage competition on public work. But what concrete benefits would be derived from the potentially cumbersome administration of the act in this manner? Although government and union officials have spoken eloquently of the act's basic purpose as preventing "the purchasing power of the federal government from being used to permit bidders on federal contracts to profit by depressing wages and working conditions,"[12] these same officials may not be as eager to support the act if prevailing wage determinations eventually come to reflect only open-shop rates. And, while many open-shop contractors admit privately that they are not against a prevailing wage law as such, just one which serves to impose a union rate, their political representatives and allies have already gone on record as supporting repeal of the act, not administrative reform. Thus, even if Davis-Bacon does represent what one Labor Department solicitor called "a fundamental principle . . . that federal procurement should not be a means of depressing local wage conditions,"[13] this principle is likely to have fewer political supporters in the future and may lose out, for better or worse, to "full and free competitive bidding."

## Notes

1. For a legislative history of the act, see Armand Thieblot, *The Davis-Bacon Act*, pp. 6-18.

2. U.S. Department of Labor, "Wage Rate Determination Procedures."

3. Business Roundtable, *Coming to Grips With Some Major Problems in the Construction Industry*, p. 25.

4. Quoted in Thieblot, *The Davis-Bacon Act*, p. 7.

5. Quoted in Arthur F. Hintze, "Taking the Waste Out of Davis-Bacon," p. 17.

6. The few, about 10 percent, that are slightly lower than the union rate are probably due to lags in reporting union wage increases or new contract terms.

7. Council on Wage and Price Stability, "An Analysis of Certain Aspects of the Administration of the Davis-Bacon Act."

8. Robert S. Goldfarb and John F. Morral III, "Cost Implications of Changing Davis-Bacon Administration," and General Accounting Office, *The Davis-Bacon Act Should Be Repealed*, chapter 6.

9. See James Blaney, "A Comparison of Occupational Structure in Union and Nonunion Residential Construction."

10. Philip Abrams, Statement for the Associated Builders and Contractors, Inc. before the Subcommittee on Housing and Urban Affairs of the Senate Committee on Banking, Housing, and Urban Affairs, May 2, 1979.

11. It might be noted that if the real purpose of Davis-Bacon and similar acts is now, as opponents claim, simply to ensure that most public work is built by union firms and workers then the U.S. Supreme Court, by not reviewing the Second Circuit Court decision in Image Carrier Corporation v. Koch, has permitted local governments to do this directly—by requiring that only union firms may bid on public contracts—rather than indirectly by regulating wages.

12. Charles Donahue, "The Davis-Bacon Act and the Walsh-Healy Act: A Comparison of Coverage and Minimum Wage Provisions." See also Robert A. Georgine, President, Building and Construction Trades Department, AFL-CIO, Testimony before the Subcomittee on Housing and Urban Affairs of the Senate Committee on Banking, Housing, and Urban Affairs, May 2, 1979.

The attempts to repeal or modify the act during 1979 brought forth an unprecedented volume of substantive literature from the Building Trades Department, AFL-CIO. A general defense of the act is contained in *The Davis-Bacon Act: It Works to Build America*; another publication, *The GAO on Davis-Bacon: A Fatally Flawed Study* critiques the GAO report. Later in 1979, the Department went further and accused the Business Roundtable, the ABC, and dual shop contractors of conspiring to "destroy the 17 building trades unions." See AFL-CIO Building Trades Department, *The Builders: Special Report* (Washington, D.C., 1979).

13. C. Donahue, "The Davis-Bacon Act . . . ," p. 513.

# 7  Institutional Response to Open-Shop Growth

Although precise measures of the relative dollar volume or employment in union and open-shop construction are difficult to obtain, the open-shop sector has clearly expanded significantly in the seventies. On the basis of the description and analysis already presented, the many reasons for this growth might be best summarized as:

1. The extreme fluctuation in the level and composition of construction volume between 1968 and 1978. This led, first, to higher union wages (and disputes) and then to the substantial unemployment of skilled workers, and, second, to entry and expansion of many smaller, open-shop firms;
2. The long-term increase in industrial and commercial building in geographic areas with less union representation;
3. The continuing evolution of technology and firm structure toward greater specialization, resulting in more substitution of equipment and materials for on-site skilled labor; and,
4. The lower total labor costs (particularly due to differences in skill and occupational mix) and greater management flexibility of many open-shop contractors.

These characteristics of the industry and of open-shop growth have now set an agendum for continued competition between the union and nonunion sectors of the industry. This competition is joined not only in the short-run competitive bidding of union versus nonunion firms, but also in the activities of other institutions in the industry. Individual firms face a long-run choice of a labor relations policy which fits their particular market context: they may choose to operate as entirely union or nonunion or, as a hedge, as a "dual shop." Employer associations must organize to bargain more effectively with the building trades unions or, if open-shop, to provide new sources of training, referral, and other services. Construction users can work to support either union or open-shop employers (or even both) in their efforts to improve on-site operations and efficiency. The building trades unions can respond in bargaining, or even unilaterally, to make union construction more competitive in particular areas or markets. Current examples of these and other types of organizational response are described below.

105

Whether any of these activities will be successful in either stabilizing the union share of the market or in sustaining further open-shop growth is still unknown. But it is clear that the very diversity of the construction industry and the sheer number of organizations in it will continue to make coherent responses to its problems difficult, if not impossible. Except for the largest, individual firms are relatively powerless to bargain for better union contracts or to implement progressive open-shop programs. Employer associations are hindered in their actions, being unstable coalitions of firms of different sizes, specialties, and labor policies. And the building trades unions themselves are fragmented among crafts, between geographic levels (international versus local) and even between union locals in one craft; and all have different perceptions of how—or whether—to respond to open-shop competition. Thus, the very fragmented structure of the industry both causes and exacerbates the difficulties in developing common and consistent labor market policies for either the union or the open-shop sectors.

**Construction Users**

Some of the recent growth in open-shop construction has been actively supported—even promoted—by both industrial and commercial users of construction. In contrast, the U.S. government, as a major user of construction, has attempted to sustain policies which keep unions predominant on some government work.

The construction cost of new plants is a major capital cost item for private industrial users of construction. As a result, they have developed the most highly organized efforts of any user group to promote cost-efficient construction. Historically, most major industrial construction projects have been carried out by union contractors. Until very recently, virtually all of the firms with the capability to design and construct major plants were union, and thus users had very little choice; also, if a user's work force was organized, the firm ran the risk of embroiling this work force in a dispute by engaging open-shop construction firms in the construction of new plants or for plant modifications or extensions.

During the late 1960s and early 1970s, several changes began to occur which made union construction less attractive to many of these industrial users. First, union construction wages leapfrogged upwards at unprecedented rates, impelled by the strong demand for construction. Second, a series of contract and other strikes paralyzed a number of major projects and created confusion and uncertainty for others. Uncertainty in schedule is intolerable to industrial clients, when they are building revenue-producing facilities in competitive markets. Third—and perhaps most significant—the shift of economic activity to the South and Southwest during the seventies meant that much of the new industrial construction was being carried out in traditionally open-shop areas, and often for users who wanted nonunion plant labor forces in the plant after construction.

Consequently, several major industrial firms began considering building their facilities with open-shop labor. After some tentative initial moves in this direction, a few major firms, notably DuPont, Dow Chemical and several oil and electric power companies, began contracting with open-shop firms for a considerable proportion of their new construction work. At the same time, representatives of the engineering departments of these large user firms began explaining the advantages of open-shop construction at industry conventions and seminars.

Nonetheless, other industrial users have elected to continue building their plants with union labor. Recognizing some of the shortcomings of local collective bargaining in construction, they have been able to avoid many local problems by having their contractors negotiate special project labor agreements which contain terms much more favorable than those in the existing local agreements. These project agreements are negotiated with all of the local unions which will be involved on the project, sometimes with the assistance of representatives from the international unions, and are binding only for the duration of the project. Typically, these will equate wages to local union wages, but will have substantially different provisions regarding such things as travel pay, shift work and overtime premiums, and the use of extra apprentices or helpers. In addition, project labor agreements have often had no-strike, no-lockout provisions. While these latter clauses insulate the industrial user from disruptions, they are particularly irksome to local union contractors who may find a major project continuing to work during a local strike and, as a result, totally undermining their own bargaining position. Thus, no-strike clauses in project agreements can solve one problem for some large union firms and their clients, only by creating another problem for local union contractors.

Industrial users have also promoted project labor agreements with open-shop construction firms, thereby keeping their construction "union." Large open-shop constructors—Daniel International is a prime example— have been able to negotiate project agreements with terms often more favorable than those in the local labor agreements, and occasionally with terms even more favorable than those in project agreements negotiated by union construction firms. The motive for the local unions to grant such extensive concessions to open-shop firms is to capture work for their union members. (Sometimes these contracts were signed even after an open-shop firm had won the contract in competition with union firms which bid the work based on the regular contract terms.) From the open-shop contractor's point of view, the project labor agreement does not tie the firm to any permanent union relationship and does provide access to the union's labor pool.

Industrial users have, therefore, found project labor agreements helpful in the short term to construct their plants "union," at a lower cost than could be obtained under the existing local labor agreements, and usually without the risk of strikes. And many local unions have been willing to make whatever concessions seem necessary to be competitive for some industrial work. At the same time, project agreements containing a no-strike, no-lockout provision can dramatically undermine the strength of the local contractors in collective bargaining. Any increases in wages and benefits which result are ultimately borne by industrial users through retroactive or future wage increases on various projects, and may also help to push up the general levels of union construction wages and benefits across the country.

In spite of such shortsighted actions as individual firms, industrial owners have attempted to influence the long-run structure and outcome of construction labor relations through an association, the Business Roundtable. The Roundtable grew out of the "National Conference on Construction Problems" sponsored by the U.S. Chamber of Commerce in the autumn of 1968 to discuss the rapidly escalating cost of industrial construction, particularly the rise in labor costs. The Chamber president at that time was Winton Blount, a large Alabama contractor, who had become convinced that contractors had serious labor relations problems, and that users were exacerbating contractors' problems by their own uninformed and self-serving actions. The conference appointed a task force of user, contractor, and contractor association members to draft proposals for action. The proposals called for the formation of "an organization of major purchasers of construction . . . to establish a responsible and informed cooperation between purchasers of construction and contractors on the construction industry's labor relations. . . ."[1]

Shortly after the issuance of a Chamber of Commerce report in 1969, the Construction Users' Anti-Inflation Roundtable was established, with Roger Blough, retired chief executive officer of U.S. Steel, as its first chairman. This group included the chief executive officers of about sixty of the nation's largest companies. A working committee of fifteen to twenty members met fortnightly in New York as the executive arm of the group.

The main thrust of "Roger's Roundtable" was to educate users about the impact their decisions could have on construction labor relations. Specifically, the Roundtable tried to dissuade its members (and other industrial users) from having their contractors continue to work through local strikes. The Roundtable stimulated the formation of independent local user groups in a number of cities to help "educate" local divisions of member companies, as well as nonmember local businesses. Their efforts are widely believed to have helped reduce—although not completely eliminate—the presence of no-strike provisions in industrial project agreements.

The Construction Users Anti-Inflation Roundtable later merged with the Labor Law Study Group (in late 1972) and other business research and lobby groups to become the Business Roundtable. In the process its scope of activities has broadened far beyond construction concerns to include general labor, environmental, taxation, welfare, and pension issues. However, the working committee of the old Roundtable lives on as the Construction Committee of the Business Roundtable and continues to be the dominant organization of construction users in the United States.

In summary, during the 1970s some industrial users supported and even promoted the open-shop sector of the industry; others have remained union, but have attempted to protect themselves from costly local agreements by encouraging their contractors to extract more favorable project labor agreements from local unions. In the latter group some owners have insisted on no-strike provisions in their project labor agreements for urgently needed facilities, in spite of the potential long-term costs of these provisions to the unionized construction industry. Whereas the Business Roundtable (1978) has helped to educate users about some of the intricacies of construction labor relations, it has had very little impact on the structure of local collective bargaining through which wages are still largely determined. Moreover, the pressures that have created high-wage settlements in local agreements can still be reinforced by the actions of some industrial users and their contractors when high construction labor costs seem to be a small price to pay for early completion of a needed facility.

In 1978, many of the international unions of the building trades signed a national agreement with a group of the largest union contractors, the National Constructors Association (NCA), which evolved from and improved upon the terms and conditions found in many previous project agreements. Called the National Industrial Construction Agreement, the contract specifies that while local wages and benefits are to be paid in an area, other conditions, such as overtime premiums and travel pay, may differ substantially. This agreement also eliminates a no-strike clause in favor of the following provision:

> In the event of an area strike over renegotiation of the local construction collective bargaining agreement, it will not be considered a violation of this agreement for the employer to stop work coming within the work jurisdiction of the striking local union, or any or all other work on the project for the duration of the strike provided that the employer gives notification to the affected unions 5 working days prior to the expiration of the local contract, or any time during the course of the strike.[2]

The inclusion of such a five-day notice clause avoids many of the undesirable and divisive aspects of no-strike, no-lockout provisions in previous contracts. This gives the national contractor the option to support other employers in a local strike, and consequently may make a local union less willing to engage in a strike.

The agreement also attempts to improve the competitiveness of union contractors on large industrial projects by instituting helpers (called "sub-journeymen") paid at 60 percent of the journeyman's base wage, and numbering up to one-third of the total employees in each trade. Although the resulting cost savings are yet to be documented, the most optimistic claims put them as high as 20 percent of labor cost, which would clearly enable union constructors to be much more cost-competitive on major industrial projects. All the provisions in this type of agreement represent union attempts to make adjustments in compensation and skill structure to be competitive for large-scale industrial work. The cost estimates in chapter 5 show that these types of provisions can have a major impact on the relative cost of union construction.

**Federal Government**

The federal government is the largest single buyer of construction services in the United States. Aside from its actions as a regulator of the industry through labor law, federal agencies have exerted some of the same kinds of pressures as private users on construction labor relations. Specifically, the U.S. Department of Transportation, under Secretary William Coleman, actively promoted the use of project labor agreements including no-strike, no-lockout provisions for mass transit construction. In fact, in approving the city of Buffalo's application for federal financing of its new mass transit system, Coleman implied that a no-strike project labor agreement between the local authority and local building trades was almost a prerequisite for federal funding of mass transit in other cities.[3] This policy was in the interests both of the local transit authorities who benefited from the reduced risk of strikes, and of large union contractors who would be working on the project. However, the measure was vigorously opposed by smaller local contractors in Buffalo, as well as in Baltimore, where an even stronger no-strike, no-lockout project agreement was negotiated. The opposition by local contractors, both union and open-shop, to these provisions was predictable. Local union contractors feared the weakening of their bargaining position as a result of the large project which could continue to operate through a local strike. Local nonunion contractors, on the other hand, found that these agreements imposed conditions on them which reduced their potential competitive advantage over union firms. For example, the Baltimore agreement, in addition to a no-strike clause, had a no-bumping clause which prevented nonunion contractors from moving their workers around between different jurisdictions.[4]

These local contractors expressed their opposition so vigorously through their national associations that Secretary Coleman backed off considerably from his initially very strong endorsement of project agreements. And in June 1977, the then-secretary, Brock Adams, stated that the appropriateness of no-strike agreements would be assessed on a case-by-case basis.[5]

A subsequent project agreement used for the construction of bus facilities in Denver modified the no-strike no-lockout provision to permit strikes in connection with local collective bargaining agreements.[6] This removed the primary objection of local contractors to these federal project agreements. Thus, local contractors who had been struggling to stem the tide of no-strike project labor agreements on private projects found some success in persuading the federal government to stop promoting their use.

**Construction Firms**

As union construction firms have perceived changes in their competitive position with open-shop firms, they have responded in ways that increase their flexibility to take advantage of potential cost savings from the open-shop form of organization.

For example, many union general contractors have had labor contracts with the trades that they customarily employ—laborers, carpenters, cement masons, ironworkers, and operating engineers—which contain subcontractor clauses. These clauses have prevented the general contractor from subcontracting with open-shop firms which employ any of these trades. This effectively limits the general's freedom to use open-shop firms on his projects. Since a very good case can be made that this restriction is necessary to prevent the general from abandoning his labor agreements (by subcontracting work to open-shop firms) whenever it suits him to do so, subcontractor clauses have been upheld by the courts as valid restraints on a general contractor's freedom to subcontract.

Thus, subcontractor clauses have historically made it difficult for union general contractors to use open-shop firms for steel erection, excavation, glazing, and other tasks, since these specialty firms use one or more of the basic trades. Over the last decade, however, a new form of contracting, the so-called construction manager (CM) concept, has introduced a new flexibility for union general contractors to use open-shop specialty firms. Under the CM form of organization, a general contractor acts as the owner's agent and helps the owner to negotiate *prime* contracts directly with all of the specialty trades. Since the general contractor has no contractual relationship with the specialty firms, the subcontractor clauses in his labor agreements have no effect. The general contractor may, therefore, recommend that the owner should use a few (or many) open-shop firms on a CM project, even though the firm is a union contractor on other projects.

The trend to construction management in commercial work is paralleled by a similar trend in industrial construction. Executives of the National Constructors Association have noted that many of their members who have previously operated as engineer-constructors now often operate as engineer-managers. This change has been at the request of owners who want the union firm's proprietary design technology or engineering skills, but also want to use open-shop constructors wherever they are less expensive.

One of the developments which has highlighted the importance of labor cost in selecting subcontractors is the increased tendency for general contractors or construction managers to purchase materials on behalf of the owner of a project, even materials customarily supplied by the specialty subcontractors. As a result, the bids from many subcontractors are now comprised almost entirely of their labor costs. To the extent that open-shop labor costs are lower, this will be more evident in their bids.

Another strategy which has been followed by union contractors in response to open-shop competition has been to create "double-breasted" firms—that is, firms with both union and open-shop components. As long as separation of the labor force and day-to-day management staffs are maintained, it is relatively easy for a construction firm to maintain two corporate entities in accord with labor law. This permits a contractor to work union when convenient, such as on projects in the center city or on publicly funded work, and to work open-shop in rural or suburban areas and on private work. Double-breasted firms can thus straddle subsectors of the construction market to ensure that competitive bids can be entered for different types and sites of work. For example, Fluor Corporation, a Los Angeles-based heavy industrial constructor, acquired Daniel International, a large nonunion firm based in Greenville, S.C., to enable them to build large industrial projects on an open-shop basis. It might be noted that while the double-breasted or dual shop form of organization may make a firm more competitive across a wider variety of construction work, it may also make it, as a union firm, less interested in forceful collective bargaining. As more work goes open-shop, the firm need not press for concessions in bargaining in order to remain competitive; it simply transfers the potential volume to its open-shop subsidiary.

**Union-Employer Associations**

One of the most innovative attempts at improving the coordination of union-contractor association activity has been the efforts of the Contractors Mutual Association (CMA). CMA was founded in May 1971 by some forty general contractors. Starting out with broad goals of improving labor relations in the industry, CMA very quickly focused its efforts in two principal areas. The first was the collection and tabulation of information on construction wages. The second was to promote coordinated wide-area bargaining in construction. By this, CMA meant that contractor associations would cooperate and coordinate bargaining with local unions across a larger area than that represented by the traditional small local. CMA also encouraged contractor associations to negotiate with a number of trades simultaneously in these wide areas. They assisted groups of local contractor associations and local unions to define larger geographic areas which corresponded to economic regions with something like a common labor pool. In spite of the difficulties of attempting to encourage contractors and unions with different and often competing objectives to bargain collectively, CMA claims credit for assisting or initiating approximately thirty of these wide-area bargaining units by 1979. Whereas the number of agreements is too small to permit substantial analysis, CMA notes that first-year increases in construction settlements for 1979 have averaged 6.2 percent in wide-area units compared with 6.6 percent in other units.[7]

Although CMA's activities were significant, the thirty wide-area bargaining units which it supported represent only a tiny percentage of all bargaining units. The vast majority of union construction agreements are still small local agreements between individual local unions and individual contractor associations or contractors. The prospects do not appear to be good that the implementation of wide-area bargaining will spread very rapidly, given the fragmented structure of construction unions and employer associations. One major reason for this is that within such wide areas, the highest union rate tends to become extended over greater distances. Thus, small firms and associations see little advantage in coordination if the results are only that the highest rate would eventually prevail across local jurisdictions and associations.

CMA's responsibilities for data collection and reporting have been taken over by four other contractor associations. Furthermore, the efforts that CMA have initiated for coordinated wide-area bargaining may be augmented (or supplanted) by the National Construction Employers Council (NCEC), the most ambitious attempt to date by union employers and their associations to coordinate labor relations policies.

The NCEC was formed in February, 1978; it evolved from the old Contractors Mutual Association and the Council of Construction Employers (CCE), an earlier attempt to coordinate construction labor relations at the national level. The NCEC is a unique effort to create an industry council, containing some twenty national associations of general and specialty contractors. Consequently, NCEC's policies must work to comprise the views of these parties who have so often disagreed in the past. NCEC's basic goal is the resolution of the industry's labor relations problems in a united way and "to restructure and bring order to the collective bargaining process."[8]

By late 1979, NCEC had moved toward this goal by holding seminars for the industry in order "to develop, coordinate and communicate common policy on collective bargaining"; and by developing a new manual for bargaining in construction containing a detailed analysis of the merits and demerits of specific labor contract clauses and their economic costs.[9]

The NCEC has also suggested local attempts by unions and contractors to cooperate in forming joint labor-management committees. Organizations such as MOST ("management and organized labor striving together") in Columbus, Ohio; PRIDE in St. Louis; and the "Union Jack" campaign in Denver represent cooperative attempts to reduce disputes on job sites and to promote the quality and efficiency of union construction to user groups. Members of MOST (twenty labor unions and ten contractor associations) signed a memorandum of understanding dedicating themselves to increasing productivity and to settling disputes without work stoppages. Certain jobs that were designated MOST projects have run on-time, under or at budget, and without stoppages. The group also used a public relations firm as an independent, impartial party to foster cooperation and also to ". . . change the image of our industry. Without PR, we could make major changes but the public wouldn't know."[10]

## Open-Shop Employer Associations

One of the most important contributions to the growth of the open shop in construction has been the role played by the Associated Builders and Contractors (ABC). Begun in the early 1950s in Maryland, ABC has expanded rapidly to become one of the largest employer associations in the industry and the largest open shop association (see figure 7-1). During the late 1960s and early 1970s its growth was particularly rapid in traditionally union geographical areas, such as the northeastern and mid-Atlantic states; since 1975 its membership has expanded in southern and western areas. Houston and Los Angeles, both traditionally strong union areas, now have the two largest ABC chapters.

ABC has been effective as an association both on the local and national levels. The staff of its local chapters concentrates on providing legal, promotional, and educational services to member firms. Local chapters also organize training and apprenticeship programs, monitor Davis-Bacon wage determinations, and operate employment referral services. The national elected leadership played an instrumental role in the defeat of the situs-picketing legislation and of labor law reform and has continually supported attempts to repeal the Davis-Bacon Act. Programs for diffusing task training systems and for creating multiemployer health and pension plans have also been developed at the national staff level.

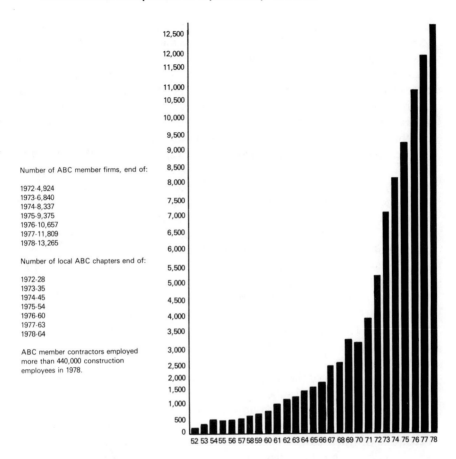

Number of ABC member firms, end of:

1972-4,924
1973-6,840
1974-8,337
1975-9,375
1976-10,657
1977-11,809
1978-13,265

Number of local ABC chapters end of:

1972-28
1973-35
1974-45
1975-54
1976-60
1977-63
1978-64

ABC member contractors employed more than 440,000 construction employees in 1978.

Source: Associated Builders and Contractors, Inc., Washington, D.C. Reprinted with permission. Statistics based on data developed for ABC by Opinion Research Corporation, Princeton, New Jersey.

**Figure 7-1**. Associated Builders and Contractors, Membership Growth, 1952-1978

ABC also represents the greatest diversity of members of virtually any employer association. Most of its members are subcontractors; the rest are either general contractors or materials suppliers. While its member firms may tend to, on average, be slightly smaller in employment and volume than the union firms, ABC's members are undoubtedly among the most substantial of the open-shop companies in open-shop commercial and industrial construction. Ironically, although it was founded on the basis of a "merit shop" philosophy which was deliberately neutral toward unions and union firms, ABC has come to represent the strongest political opposition to unions in the industry. Indeed, one of the major services ABC provides its individual members is the support and strength gained by the mutual association of many firms against perceived discrimination by government bureaucracies and pressures by local unions. As ABC becomes as successful in providing a range of services to its member firms (particularly in the area of training and apprenticeship) as it has been in political leadership, the capabilities of the open-shop sector will be substantially enhanced.

Perhaps recognizing this, the president-elect of ABC for the 1980 term, Ted C. Kennedy, has emphasized the importance of expanding the Association's efforts in training and has reaffirmed ABC's commitment to the merit-shop philosophy. In terms of training, ABC looks to the expansion of the modular craft training programs (described in chapter 4), the flexibility of which would permit the training of craft journeymen and the cross-training of helpers. Kennedy noted that if the Labor Department withholds the official approval of these programs that is necessary to certify apprentices, and "maintains that it has to use old, archaic programs and follow traditional craft guidelines, then we'll have to go to court." But Kennedy also spoke of trying to modify ABC's image as a nonunion or anti-union association. He commented, "I think that most of ABC's general contractor members are truly merit shop in that they do subcontract work to union contractors . . . the unions would have hurt themselves if they were able to force repeal of the situs picketing prohibitions. Merit Shop contractors would have stopped subcontracting union firms."[11]

Another association which now competes with ABC to represent nonunion general contractors is the Associated General Contractors (AGC). Indeed, one of the dramatic changes that have taken place over the last few years has been the rapid growth in open-shop membership of the AGC, which was previously largely union. Historically, AGC's major emphasis has been devoted to bargaining on behalf of local general contractors with the local unions of the basic trades. While the AGC has been the most effective local and national association of union contractors, by July 1979 more than forty percent of AGC's membership was open-shop. Now, as AGC's open-shop membership continues to expand, its goals and priorities may have to change accordingly. It is in the unenviable position of representing the interests of what can be two dramatically opposed groups: union and nonunion firms. At the national level, this creates obvious difficulties in formulating positions on laws and legislation, such as Davis-Bacon or situs picketing, which work to the advantage of some of its members and to the disadvantage of others.[12] At the local level, the AGC represents in bargaining most of the larger union conractors, many of whom may operate open-shop subsidiaries. The interest of these dual-shop firms in pressing for concessions from the unions may be tempered somewhat by their belief that the business of their open-shop subsidiaries can expand as the competitiveness of their union firms declines.

In summary, construction employers, acting individually as contractors or jointly with other firms or user groups, have had three options in responding to nonunion growth. First, they can "go open shop" and work to expand the volume of their nonunion business as well as to cooperate with other nonunion employers in lobbying for changes in legislation which are favorable to the open shop. Second, union firms can engage in strong and concerted efforts to improve bargaining in construction so that labor costs are reduced and union companies remain competitive. Third, union contractors can join with the building trades in cooperative efforts to promote union construction and to defeat the legislative initiatives of the open shop. There has been activity along all of these lines in the construction industry in the 1970s; no doubt it will intensify in the future. But what makes the political and economic environment of change in construction so turbulent is that many union employers and their associations are following all three of these policies at the same time. While the coincidence of hard bargaining and labor-management cooperation is not new in construction, it is now more difficult for union employers to succeed in either or both of these efforts if they are also operating nonunion or supporting the open shop on the side. As a result, construction employer associations could become completely polarized in the near future, despite the continuing attempts to sustain them as union and open-shop coalitions, as in the AGC or even the ABC. Such polarization can make efforts directed toward bargaining reform (not to mention union-management cooperation) difficult or impossible.

**The Building Trades Unions**

Many union construction firms can use their corporate flexibility to adapt and survive in the face of growing open-shop competition. They do this by changing the type or size of contracts they bid or by starting a nonunion subsidiary. Individual union members can also adjust to nonunion growth. Many have "put their union card in their shoe" and gone to work for open-shop firms—particularly during periods of high unemployment in the industry. In fact, it has been relatively easy for individual union members to work on open-shop projects at lower wage rates when there was insufficient demand for work at the union wage-scale. But unlike private corporations or individual union members, the building trades unions as institutions do not have these alternatives. They must react to increased competition in construction while remaining committed to traditional union goals. Of course, one form of adjustment they can make is to supplement their membership through diversification; whether union construction employment is declining or not, new members can be organized in other industries. Many of the buildings trades unions have grown in just this manner during the 1970s.

Nonetheless, construction membership still represents by far the largest proportion of the building trades constituents and they have attempted to respond to the needs of this membership in various ways. By the end of the 1970s, the following types of institutional response could be observed:

First, the rate of increase in union wages in construction has been moderate throughout the 1970s in most regions of the country. Between 1976 and 1979, the annual average rate of change in building trades agreements was roughly 6 percent—equivalent to, if not slightly less than, the rate of inflation as measured by the Consumer Price Index. Although the rate of increase jumped to about 8 percent during 1979, it still lagged behind price increases by a large margin. Of course, given the well-established responsiveness of construction wages to industry unemployment, this relative moderation should not have been unexpected or attributed completely to nonunion competition.[13] The change in the rate of wage increase, like many of the other measures we will discuss, was as much a function of the deep recession in the industry as it was of the growth of the open shop.

Second, in areas of particular economic distress or intense nonunion activity, construction unions have adopted wage freezes, on an individual or multitrade basis. For example, in Washington, D.C. a multicraft agreement in early 1978 provided for a wage freeze and other concessions on showup pay, overtime premiums, and work rules. In Mobile in 1978, ten crafts signed a two-year agreement for no wage increase coupled with a decrease in overtime premiums in response to nonunion competition and in awareness of the substantial compensation increases in previous contracts. The employer's representative commented, "I can't give enough credit to the union business agents who saw the light and understood what had to be done."[14] But attempts by local business agents and the international union to make substantial concessions in a bricklayers' contract in New York City led to wildcat strikes and multiple law suits, because of resistance of the local membership. Although in this case a contract was finally signed which incorporated some unimportant modifications, the ability of unions to make such rapid and drastic changes in contract terms even under severe economic pressure clearly varies across trades, locals, and areas.

Third, as described earlier, local and national project agreements have been developed to adapt union wages, work rules, labor requirements, skill ratios, and even jurisdictional boundaries to particular circumstances or types of work. In Michigan, after a $20 million refinery was built largely by open-shop contractors (who may, nonetheless, have employed union members), ten building trades unions signed a project agreement for the construction of a $1.5 million addition which reduced overtime premiums, eliminated travel pay, prohibited strikes, gave employers total authority to determine crew size and worker requirements for all jobs, and provided makeup work time at straight hourly wages. At the national level, new agreements have been signed which cover many large industrial projects (between the National Constructors Association and various building trade unions) or nuclear power plants (between the same unions and several large construction firms) and which provide similar concessions in work conditions on a uniform national basis.

Fourth, some unions, such as the United Association of Plumbers and Pipefitters and the Sheetmetal Workers, have also attempted to establish special wage rates and conditions for smaller-scale commercial work. Ed Carlough, president of the Sheetmetal Workers, has encouraged locals of that union to adopt flexible work rules and different wages and conditions for "specialty" sheetmetal work such as metal buildings; metal ceilings and partitions; flashings, gutters, and downspouts; and "all other sheetmetal specialty work" being performed by nonunion shops. He commented, "We have attempted to maintain the same wages and conditions in the specialty sector that apply to work in the HVAC [heating, ventilating, and air conditioning] sector of our union. We must now face up to the problem and to the challenge, and do so by changing our approach to the problem."[15] Representing quite a different policy, but with similar goals, President Martin Ward of the United Association (UA) has attempted to restructure union locals in some areas both to reduce interlocal competition in wages ("leapfrogging") and to establish locals based on the type of construction on which the union members work instead of assigning membership in a local union on the basis of a craftsman's skills (in plumbing, say, or pipefitting). Ward was also instrumental in creating a national UA industrial agreement which established a subjourneyman classification to permit less-skilled workers to be hired at lower wage rates. This provision was subsequently incorporated into the two national agreements previously discussed. Other unions, such as the Bricklayers' and the Carpenters', have also taken steps to reduce the number of small locals, particularly in urban areas in the East. This reduction increases the financial resources for local union administration and enlarges the geographic mobility of union journeymen and contractors.

It should be noted, of course, that these attempts by some of the presidents of the building trades unions to influence and moderate the terms of local bargaining and settlements are not new. Indeed, one of the reasons for the success of the Construction Industry Stabilization Committee in the early 1970s was the cooperation of the Internationals. Yet, the political autonomy of the union locals continues to make central influence on wages and conditions difficult to implement. The new national agreements are a major breakthrough in the structure of construction bargaining that reduces local autonomy: they may foreshadow increasing centralization of bargaining processes and some moderation of outcomes.[16]

Fifth, in contrast to these measures, all of which work to make the building trades more competitive in particular types of construction, the unions have also taken various offensive measures. One of the most important was the renewed attempt to pass situs-picketing legislation in order to concentrate union market power through the picketing of entire construction sites. If this legislation had been successful, it would have counterbalanced the current ability of general contractors to subcontract more work to open-shop firms.[17] Another innovation has been the creation of an organizing effort within the Building Trades Department of the AFL-CIO. This has had some reported success in enlisting new union members in two target cities, Baltimore and Los Angeles, but no open-shop firms as entities have yet been organized. Interestingly enough, the organizing literature in this effort celebrates the very union wages and jurisdictions which are being modified in some other union agreements. The unions have also resorted to mass demonstrations at open-shop project sites and to pressure on union contractors who work on open-shop jobs. Individual union members have been involved in scattered acts of vandalism and violence against open-shop sites and contractors.

In sum, the competitive responses by unions in construction might be characterized in two ways. First, they represent one side of a dynamic process of adjustment to labor market conditions in which unions appear to alternate between an emphasis on wage gains and, after a lag, a concern for employment levels—rather than making some static trade-off between these two goals, as is usually assumed in academic theories of union behavior. Second, they represent an evolution of union policy in construction from the goal of maintaining relatively common wages and conditions across many subsections of the industry toward a strategy of greater differentiation of contract terms to fit the competitive conditions in different product markets. Although in the past, the building trades unions and their employers may have been willing to give up employment in subsectors, such as residential construction, where the skill levels and degree of interfirm competition did not support substantial levels of compensation and profits, the continuance of this type of policy by the building trades unions might eventually lead to very low levels of employment in only a few types of construction. An alternate strategy permits the union to act like a discriminating monopolist and maintain higher levels of employment in various product markets by establishing differentiated wages, skills, and contract conditions. Of course, as for the discriminating monopolist in the product market, such policies create tensions between market segments and provide incentives for employers (or some workers) to cheat by avoiding market segmentation rules.

At present, there is no indication of how successful any of the adjustments made by union employers or the building trades unions will be in preventing further erosion of work to open-shop firms. The continuation of major cyclical fluctuations in construction volume, coupled with increasing capital investment in nonunion areas, will certainly give a basic advantage to nonunion contractors. But if open-shop firms do come to dominate the market for commercial and industrial construction, they may have to create common institutions or programs for the training, referral, and compensation of skilled and semiskilled workers. If many open-shop employees find they are unfairly treated in those programs or denied a voice in the design of labor policies, the industry might again become highly organized, but perhaps on a multicraft or "industrial" basis.

## Notes

1. Chamber of Commerce of the U.S. "National Conference on Construction Problems," Task Force Report, July 1979.

2. NCA, and several building trades unions, National Industrial Construction Agreement, 1978.

3. *Engineering News-Record*, June 17, 1976, p. 11.

4. *Construction Labor Report*, No. 1008, September 1, 1976, p. A-19.

5. *Construction Labor Report*, No. 1129, June 22, 1977, p. A-13.

6. *Engineering News-Record*, August 18, 1977, p. 84.

7. These figures, as well as a comprehensive description and analysis of CMA, can be found in Donald Cullen and Louis Feinberg, *The Bargaining Structure in Construction: Problems and Prospects*, (January, 1979, n.p.).

8. *Engineering News-Record*, February 15, 1979, p. 36.

9. *Engineering News-Record*, October 11, 1979, p. 64 and October 25, 1979, p. 78.

10. *Engineering News-Record*, July 19, 1979, p. 94.

11. *Engineering News-Record*, October 18, 1979, pp. 31, 34 and generally in interviews with ABC national presidents, national staff, and ten chapter directors and staff from 1976 through 1979.

12. *Engineering News-Record*, "AGC Closes Ranks on Davis-Bacon," October 18, 1979, p. 65, describes dissension at an AGC board meeting over Davis-Bacon. Some contractors held that the law was vital to the survival of union contractors, but AGC's position of "repeal or modification" was reaffirmed.

13. On the impact of unemployment on construction wages, see D.Q. Mills, "Wage Determination in Contract Construction," *Industrial Relations*, February 1971.

14. *Construction Labor Report*, No. 1203, August 23, 1978, p. A-16.

15. Construction Labor Report, No. 1174, July 10, 1978, p. A-22.

16. One outgrowth of the successful experience of the Construction Industry Stabilization Committee in the early 1970s was the incorporation of a proposal for a "Construction Industry Collective Bargaining Committee" in the proposed situs-picketing legislation of 1975. See Cullen and Feinberg, op. cit., pp. 159-163, and *Construction Labor Report*, December 10, 1975, Section H. The latter committee would have enabled the international unions to exert more control over local bargaining.

17. A recent decision of the 9th Circuit U.S. Court of Appeals has further eroded the unions' ability to limit open-shop subcontracting through "subcontractor clauses" in their labor agreements. See *Construction Labor Report*, January 9, 1980, p. A-13.

# Appendix A
# Survey Methodology
# and Instruments

The 1976 survey from which much of the source material for this study was drawn had two components. The first was a wage questionnaire mailed to a large random sample of all contractors in each of eight selected metropolitan areas: Atlanta, Baltimore, Boston, Denver, Grand Rapids, Kansas City, Portland (Oregon) and New Orleans. The format and content of the questionnaires are described in chapter 3. The universe of firms from which the sample was drawn was constructed by combining Dun and Bradstreet listings of firms in construction with membership lists from all the significant contractor associations. Since no prior identification of firms by union or nonunion status was possible, the sample could not be stratified along that dimension. To preserve the confidentiality of the responses, questionnaires were returned anonymously. Firms which mailed questionnaires also returned postcards separately. A followup mailing was then sent to nonrespondents. After this, remaining nonrespondents were again surveyed and their responses were tabulated to ascertain if a nonresponse adjustment factor was needed. Since there was, at conventional confidence levels, no significant differences between the mean wages in the two surveys, the original survey results were tabulated to provide mean wages and other data for union and nonunion firms.

Table A-1 provides information on the universe of firms, the sample, and the response rate. Although the final response rate is low (roughly 20 percent), it is comparable to other mail surveys of this type. Tables B-1 through B-8 in appendix B contain the wage and benefit data by area, occupation, and union or nonunion status. (These tables also report the Davis-Bacon wage determination in effect at the time of the survey.) It might be noted that the results of this survey as reported in those tables are consistent with the finding of the BLS surveys (1978) of wages in construction undertaken in similar areas at the same time.

The second component of the survey was the completion of 240 interview schedules (see appendix C) with both union and open-shop firms in the eight metropolitan areas. Here the sample of contractors interviewed was not random; direct referrals to firms of different sizes and types were provided through contacts with the local directors of various employers associations—most often, by AGC and ABC. The interview schedule was designed to be both comprehensive and open-ended. Its purpose was simply to elicit information on current operating practices of construction firms. These interview results provide the source for the descriptive material in chapter 4 as well as a basis for generating new hypotheses about the nature and impact of various work practices in construction.

**Table A-1**
**1976 Wage Survey Sample**

| Standard Metropolitan Statistical Area | Number of Firms | Number Mailed | Number Responded |
|---|---|---|---|
| Atlanta | 7,023 | 2,284 | 298 |
| Baltimore | 4,056 | 1,980 | 386 |
| Boston | 6,058 | 2,413 | 481 |
| Denver | 4,338 | 1,680 | 418 |
| Grand Rapids | 1,809 | 830 | 205 |
| Kansas City | 3,821 | 1,117 | 220 |
| New Orleans | 3,538 | 1,450 | 177 |
| Portland, Oregon | 3,815 | 1,602 | 375 |
| Total | 34,458 | 13,700 | 2,560 |

**Appendix B
Mean Wages by
Occupation and
Product Market,
1976 Survey**

**Table B-1**
**Atlanta, Georgia**

| Trade | Nonunion[a] | | | Union[b] | | | Percent Union Wage Differential (Building) | Davis-Bacon[b] | |
|---|---|---|---|---|---|---|---|---|---|
| | Building | Residential | Heavy and Highway | Building | Residential | Heavy and Highway | | Commercial | Residential |
| **Bricklayer** | | | | | | | | | |
| Journeyman | 6.88 (.11) | 5.13 (.14) | 4.56 (.23) | 8.85(.95) | | | 29 | 8.85(1.00) | 7.01 |
| Helper | 5.17 (.07) | 3.69 (.11) | — | | | | | | |
| **Carpenter** | | | | | | | | | |
| Journeyman | 6.6 (.08) | 6.10 (.09) | 4.40 (.07) | 8.75(.85) | | | 31 | 8.75(.97) | 5.02 |
| Helper | 4.29 (.09) | 3.62 (.09) | — | | | | | | |
| **Electrician** | | | | | | | | | |
| Journeyman | 5.94 (.12) | 5.63 (.21) | — | 9.95(1.68) | 6.20(1.06) | | 68 | 9.95(1.74) | 6.20(1.40) |
| Helper | 4.16 (.10) | 3.45 (.11) | — | | | | | | |
| **Ironworker** | | | | | | | | | |
| Journeyman | 6.30 (.20) | 5.75 (.15) | — | 8.60(1.02) | | | 37 | 8.60(1.09) | 4.26 |
| Helper | 5.61 (.25) | — | — | | | | | | |
| **Operating Engineer** | | | | | | | | | |
| Journeyman | 6.29 (.35) | — | 5.29 (.15) | 8.85(.60) | | | 41 | 8.50(1.02) | 4.58 |
| Helper | 3.55 (.19) | — | 3.75 | | | | | | |
| **Painter** | | | | | | | | | |
| Journeyman | 6.81 (.43) | 6.21 (.31) | — | 8.70(1.00) | | | 28 | 8.70(.99) | 5.38 |
| Helper | 4.17 (.18) | 4.35 (.21) | — | | | | | | |

| | | | | | | | |
|---|---|---|---|---|---|---|---|
| **Plumbers and Pipefitters** | | | | | | | |
| Journeyman | 6.47 (.14) | 6.13 (.12) | — | 9.95(1.15) | 54 | 9.95(1.26) | 9.80/1.06 |
| Helper | 3.64 (.10) | 3.77 (.10) | — | — | | | |
| **Roofer** | | | | | | | |
| Journeyman | 6.62 (.04) | 5.25 (.43) | — | 6.75(.50) | 2 | 7.00(.50) | 4.86 |
| Helper | 4.90 (.07) | 3.25 — | — | — | | | |
| **Sheet Metal Worker** | | | | | | | |
| Journeyman | 6.17 (.12) | 5.04 (.13) | — | 9.65(.91) | 56 | 9.40(1.22) | 4.47 |
| Helper | 3.63 (.06) | 3.22 (.07) | — | — | | | |
| **Truck Driver** | | | | | | | |
| Journeyman | — | — | — | 6.15(.15) | | 4.00 | 3.37 |
| Helper | — | — | — | — | | | |
| **Laborer** | | | | | | | |
| Journeyman | 3.97 (.06) | 5.33 (.24) | 3.77 (.10) | 5.65(.40) | 42 | 5.80(.50) | 3.31 |
| Helper | — | — | — | — | | | |

Mean Differential: 39%
Range: 2% to 68%

Source: 1976 survey by the Department of Housing and Urban Development and the Massachusetts Institute of Technology.

[a]Hourly wage only, excluding benefits. Standard errors in parentheses.

[b]Basic hourly wage. Hourly benefits in parentheses.

**Table B-2**
**Baltimore, Maryland**

| Trade | Nonunion[a] | | | Union[b] | | | Percent Union Wage Differential (Building) | Davis-Bacon[b] | |
|---|---|---|---|---|---|---|---|---|---|
| | Building | Residential | Heavy and Highway | Building | Residential | Heavy and Highway | | Commercial | Residential |
| Bricklayer | | | | | | | | | |
| Journeyman | 7.81 (.15) | 5.13 (.14) | 6.25 (.40) | 9.95(1.20) | 8.35(1.00) | | 27 | 10.15(1.07) | 7.50 |
| Helper | 5.50 (.14) | 3.69 (.11) | — | | | | | | |
| Carpenter | | | | | | | | | |
| Journeyman | 6.72 (.08) | 6.10 (.09) | — | 9.80(1.44) | | | 46 | 9.80(1.49) | 5.90 |
| Helper | 5.00 (.03) | 3.62 (.09) | — | | | | | | |
| Electrician | | | | | | | | | |
| Journeyman | 6.40 (.11) | 5.63 (.21) | — | 10.20(1.50) | 6.00(.96) | | 59 | 10.00(1.30) | 6.23 |
| Helper | 3.95 (.16) | 3.45 (.11) | — | | | | | | |
| Ironworker | | | | | | | | | |
| Journeyman | 6.58 (.32) | 5.75 (.15) | — | 9.77(2.33) | | | 49 | 9.77(2.39) | 6.52 |
| Helper | — | — | — | | | | | | |
| Operating Engineer | | | | | | | | | |
| Journeyman | 5.50 (.13) | — | 5.70 (.10) | 10.38(1.00) | | | 89 | 10.25(1.60) | 5.37 |
| Helper | 3.75 (.31) | — | — | | | | | | |

| | | | | | | | |
|---|---|---|---|---|---|---|---|
| **Painter** | | | | | | | |
| Journeyman | 6.73 (.14) | 6.21 (.31) | — | 9.20(1.35) | 37 | 9.20(1.41) | 5.69 |
| Helper | 5.50 (.23) | 4.35 (.21) | — | | | | |
| **Plumbers and Pipefitters** | | | | | | | |
| Journeyman | 6.50 (.15) | 6.13 (.12) | — | 10.48(1.50) | 61 | 10.93(1.05) | 5.97 |
| Helper | 4.84 (.12) | 3.79 (.11) | — | 10.93(.75) | | | |
| **Roofer** | | | | | | | |
| Journeyman | 7.21 (.48) | 5.25 (.43) | — | 7.90(.75) | 10 | 7.90(.80) | 5.45 |
| Helper | 4.94 (.37) | 3.25 | — | | | | |
| **Sheetmetal Worker** | | | | | | | |
| Journeyman | 6.23 (.08) | 5.04 (.13) | — | 11.57 | n.a. | 10.12(1.50) | 5.61 |
| Helper | 4.21 (.12) | 3.22 (.07) | — | | | | |
| **Truck Driver** | | | | | | | |
| Journeyman | 5.29 (.09) | — | 5.37 (.12) | 8.90(1.20) | 68 | 7.74(1.40) | 4.00 |
| Helper | | | | | | | |
| **Laborer** | | | | | | | |
| Journeyman | 4.60 (.06) | 5.33 (.24) | — | | n.a. | 7.00(.875) | 3.95 |
| Helper | | | | | | | |

**Mean Differential: 50%**

**Range: 27% to 89%**

Source: 1976 survey by the Department of Housing and Urban Development and the Massachusetts Institute of Technology.

Note: n.a. means not available.

[a]Hourly wage only, excluding benefits. Standard errors in parentheses.

[b]Basic hourly wage. Hourly benefits in parentheses.

**Table B-3**
**Boston, Massachusetts**

| Trade | Nonunion[a] | | | Union[b] | | | Percent Union Wage Differential (Building) | Davis-Bacon[b] | |
|---|---|---|---|---|---|---|---|---|---|
| | Building | Residential | Heavy and Highway | Building | Residential | Heavy and Highway | | Commercial | Residential |
| **Bricklayer** | | | | | | | | | |
| Journeyman | 7.78 (.30) | 7.04 (.16) | — | 9.90(1.75) | | | 27 | 9.90(2.04) | 9.90(2.04) |
| Helper | 6.13 (.45) | 4.95 (.28) | — | | | | | | |
| **Carpenter** | | | | | | | | | |
| Journeyman | 8.19 (.19) | 6.73 (.13) | — | 10.00(1.60) | | | 22 | 10.00(1.33) | 10.00(1.33) |
| Helper | 5.20 (.24) | 4.23 (.14) | — | | | | | | |
| **Electrician** | | | | | | | | | |
| Journeyman | 6.21 (.08) | 6.55 (.25) | — | 11.25(2.16) | | | 50 | 10.75(1.90) | 10.75(1.90) |
| Helper | 3.83 (.08) | 4.56 (.26) | — | | | | | | |
| **Ironworker** | | | | | | | | | |
| Journeyman | 6.29 (.52) | — | — | 10.49(2.20) | | 12.69 | 67 | 9.99(2.56) | 9.99(2.56) |
| Helper | 3.13 (.33) | — | — | | | | | | |
| **Operating Engineer** | | | | | | | | | |
| Journeyman | 9.12 (.67) | 6.75 (.19) | 11.07 (.59) | 10.61(1.90) | | 12.00/0.77 | 16 | 10.61(1.92) | 10.61(1.92) |
| Helper | 3.42 (.54) | 3.75 | — | | | | | | |
| **Painter** | | | | | | | | | |
| Journeyman | 5.64 (.09) | 6.83 (.32) | — | 9.76(1.77) | | | 73 | 9.46(1.61) | 8.61(1.59) |
| Helper | 4.32 (.26) | 3.67 (.07) | — | | | | | | |

| | | | | | | | |
|---|---|---|---|---|---|---|---|
| Plumbers and Pipefitters | | | | | | | |
| Journeyman | 7.31 (.32) | 7.12 (.16) | 8.43 (.05) | Pl 10.80(2.30) pp 11.76(1.94) | Pl 48 | 10.25(1.33) | 10.25(1.33) |
| Helper | 4.88 (.57) | 4.34 (.29) | | | | | |
| Roofer | | | | | | | |
| Journeyman | 7.34 (.15) | — | — | 9.75(1.90) | 33 | 9.75(1.55) | 9.75(1.55) |
| Helper | 5.07 (.11) | — | — | | | | |
| Sheetmetal Worker | | | | | | | |
| Journeyman | 8.08 (.49) | | — | 12.39 total | — | 9.93(2.02) | 9.93(2.02) |
| Helper | 3.82 (.2752) | | — | | | | |
| Truck Driver | | | | | | | |
| Journeyman | 5.38 (.11) | 6.79 (.18) | 8.75 (.26) | 8.11(.85) | 51 | 7.44(1.12) | 7.44(1.12) |
| Helper | | | | | | | |
| Laborer | | | | | | | |
| Journeyman | 6.10 | 5.42 | 7.19 | 7.50(1.35) | 23 | 7.50(1.05) | 7.50(1.05) |
| Helper | | | | 8.95 total | | | |

**Mean Differential: 41%**
**Range: 16% to 73%**

Source: 1976 survey by the Department of Housing and Urban Development and the Massachusetts Institute of Technology.
[a]Hourly wage only, excluding benefits. Standard errors in parentheses.
[b]Basic hourly wage. Hourly benefits in parentheses.

**Table B-4**
**Denver/Boulder, Colorado**

| Trade | Nonunion[a] | | | Union[b] | | | Percent Union Wage Differential (Building) | Davis-Bacon[b] | |
|---|---|---|---|---|---|---|---|---|---|
| | Building | Residential | Heavy and Highway | Building | Residential | Heavy and Highway | | Commercial | Residential |
| Bricklayer | | | | | | | | | |
| Journeyman | 7.97 (.33) | 7.47 (.17) | — | 9.95(1.30) | | | 25 | 9.70(1.60) (Denver) 9.10(1.35) (Boulder) | 8.25(1.35) (Denver) 7.70(1.00) (Boulder) |
| Helper | 6.25 (.60) | 4.72 (.09) | — | | | | | | |
| Carpenter | | | | | | | | | |
| Journeyman | 6.95 (.12) | 6.09 (.05) | — | 9.19(1.73) | 6.15(1.98) | 8.54(1.98) | 32 | 9.035(2.04) | 7.465 |
| Helper | 4.62 (.13) | 3.87 (.06) | — | | | | | | |
| Electrician | | | | | | | | | |
| Journeyman | 7.66 (.17) | 6.60 (.29) | — | 10.94(1.31) | 7.20(.64) | | 43 | 10.94(1.20) | 6.75c(.37) (Denver) 6.30c(.37) (Boulder) |
| Helper | 4.36 (.23) | 4.00 (.37) | — | | | | | | |
| Ironworker | | | | | | | | | |
| Journeyman | 6.94 (.16) | 6.88 (.07) | — | 9.75(1.86) | | | 41 | 9.75(1.96) | None |
| Helper | 6.27 (.29) | 4.25 | | | | | | | |
| Operating Engineer | | | | | | | | | |
| Journeyman | 6.97 (.24) | 6.22 (.19) | 6.23 (.30) | 8.50(1.54) | | | 22 | 8.35(1.60) | 5.90(.55) (Front-end loader) |
| Helper | 5.66 (.22) | 3.75 (.15) | — | | | | | | |
| Painter | | | | | | | | | |
| Journeyman | 7.00 (.34) | 6.43 (.23) | — | 10.04(1.10) | | | 43 | 9.76(1.96) | 7.41(.56) |
| Helper | 4.25 | 3.86 (.14) | — | | | | | | |

| | | | | | | |
|---|---|---|---|---|---|---|
| **Plumbers and Pipefitters** | | | | | | |
| Journeyman | 6.12 (.26) | 6.91 (.21) | 10.30(1.75) | Pl 68 | 10.15(2.00) (Denver) 10.30(1.85) (Boulder) | 8.05(1.50) |
| Helper | 3.77 (.03) | 4.34 (.29) | — | | | |
| **Roofer** | | | | | | |
| Journeyman | 8.42 (.25) | 5.15 (.38) | 9.41(.95) | 12 | 9.81(1.38) | 7.65(.39) |
| Helper | 4.13 (.12) | 3.55 (.11) | — | | | |
| **Sheetmetal Worker** | | | | | | |
| Journeyman | 8.51 (.28) | 6.86 (.19) | 10.67(1.91) | 25 | 11.06(1.63) | 8.47(1.02) |
| Helper | 3.80 (.23) | 4.42 (.12) | — | | | |
| **Truck Driver** | | | | | | |
| Journeyman | — | 6.11 (.13) | 7.55(.40) | — | 7.80(1.15) | 5.10(.60) |
| Helper – | — | — | — | | | |
| **Laborer** | | | | | | |
| Journeyman | 5.73 (.22) | 4.33 (.08) | 6.35(.94) | 11 | 7.00(1.09) | 3.87 |
| Helper | — | — | — | | | |

Mean Differential: 40%
Range: 11% to 68%

Source: 1976 survey by the Department of Housing and Urban Development and the Massachusetts Institute of Technology.

[a]Hourly wage only, excluding benefits. Standard errors in parentheses.
[b]Basic hourly wage. Hourly benefits in parentheses.
[c]Not to exceed three full stories.

**Table B-5**
**Grand Rapids, Michigan**

| Trade | Nonunion[a] | | | Union[b] | | | Percent Union Wage Differential (Building) | Davis-Bacon[b] | |
|---|---|---|---|---|---|---|---|---|---|
| | Building | Residential | Heavy and Highway | Building | Residential | Heavy and Highway | | Commercial | Residential |
| Bricklayer | | | | | | | | | |
| Journeyman | 6.44 (.13) | 6.20 (.09) | — | 9.60 total | 7.72 total | | 49 | 7.70(.54) | 5.00 |
| Helper | 5.06 (.10) | 4.91 (.05) | — | | | | | | |
| Carpenter | | | | | | | | | |
| Journeyman | 5.70 (.08) | 5.63 (.11) | — | 8.85(1.10) | | | 55 | 6.23 | 4.25 |
| Helper | 4.25 (.16) | 4.54 (.27) | — | | | | | | |
| Electrician | | | | | | | | | |
| Journeyman | 6.63 (.13) | 5.75 (.17) | — | 9.62(.85) | 6.35(.46) | | 45 | 9.62(.76) | 4.50 |
| Helper | 3.35 (.09) | — | — | | | | | | |
| Ironworker | | | | | | | | | |
| Journeyman | 6.28 (.18) | — | — | | | | | 6.43 | 3.75 |
| Helper | 5.54 (.24) | — | — | | | | | | |
| Operating Engineer | | | | | | | | | |
| Journeyman | 5.44 (.12) | — | 7.25 (—) | | | | | 8.70(1.12) | 5.37 |
| Helper | — | — | — | | | | | | |

| Trade / Position | | | | | | |
| --- | --- | --- | --- | --- | --- | --- |
| **Painter** | | | | | | |
| Journeyman | 5.59 (.11) | — | — | | 6.70 | 4.78 |
| Helper | 3.75 (.12) | — | — | | | |
| **Plumbers and Pipefitters** | | | | | | |
| Journeyman | 7.11 (.13) | 6.11 (.13) | 10.64(1.30) | 50 | 9.59(.73) | 5.57 |
| Helper | 5.25 (.18) | — | — | | | |
| **Roofer** | | | | | | |
| Journeyman | — | — | 6.85(.95) | | 5.14 | 3.60 |
| Helper | — | — | — | | | |
| **Sheetmetal Worker** | | | | | | |
| Journeyman | 6.50 (.31) | 5.40 (.15) | 10.64 total | 64 | 7.50(1.24) | 4.75 |
| Helper | 4.17 (.07) | 4.00 (.28) | — | | | |
| **Truck Driver** | | | | | | |
| Journeyman | — | — | — | | 5.80 | 5.98 |
| Helper | — | — | — | | | |
| **Laborer** | | | | | | |
| Journeyman | 5.03 (.26) | 5.96 (.33) | — | | 5.81(1.29) | 3.56 |
| Helper | | | | | | |

**Mean Differential: 52%**
**Range: 45% to 64%**

Source: 1976 survey by the Department of Housing and Urban Development and the Massachusetts Institute of Technology.

[a]Hourly wage only, excluding benefits. Standard errors in parentheses.

[b]Basic hourly wage. Hourly benefits in parentheses.

**Table B-6**
**Kansas City, Missouri**

| | Nonunion[a] | | | Union[b] | | | | Davis-Bacon[b] | |
| Trade | Building | Residential | Heavy and Highway | Building | Residential | Heavy and Highway | Percent Union Wage Differential (Building) | Commercial | Residential |
|---|---|---|---|---|---|---|---|---|---|
| Bricklayer | | | | | | | | | |
| Journeyman | — | — | | | | | | 9.725(1.90) | 9.725(1.90) |
| Helper | — | — | | | | | | | |
| Carpenter | | | | | | | | | |
| Journeyman | — | 8.75 (.66) | | 10.20(.63) | 9.70(.63) | | | 10.20(.85) | 9.70(.85) |
| Helper | — | — | | | | | | | |
| Electrician | | | | | | | | | |
| Journeyman | — | — | | | | | | 10.62(1.46) | 8.01(1.40) |
| Helper | — | — | | | | | | | |
| Ironworker | | | | | | | | | |
| Journeyman | — | — | | | | | | 9.60(2.75) | 9.60(2.75) |
| Helper | — | — | | | | | | | |
| Operating Engineer | | | | | | | | | |
| Journeyman | — | — | | | | | | 10.10(2.35) | 10.10(2.35) |
| Helper | — | — | | | | | | | |

| Trade | | | | |
|---|---|---|---|---|
| **Painter** | | | | |
| Journeyman | – | – | 9.49(1.32) | 9.49(1.32) |
| Helper | – | – | | |
| **Plumbers and Pipefitters** | | | | |
| Journeyman | – | – | 11.64(1.56) | 10.69(1.40) |
| Helper | – | – | | |
| **Roofer** | | | | |
| Journeyman | – | – | 9.80(1.09) | 9.30(.94) |
| Helper | – | – | | |
| **Sheetmetal Worker** | | | | |
| Journeyman | – | – | 11.355(1.05) | 10.705(.90) |
| Helper | – | – | | |
| **Truck Driver** | | | | |
| Journeyman | – | – | 3.575(1.50) | 8.575(1.50) |
| Helper | – | – | | |
| **Laborer** | | | | |
| Journeyman | 7.58 | 8.10(1.35) | 8.10(1.45) | 8.10(1.45) |
| Helper | – | | | |

Source: 1976 survey by the Department of Housing and Urban Development and the Massachusetts Institute of Technology.

Note: Lack of comparative tabulations is a function of the small amount of nonunion activity.

[a] Hourly wage only, excluding benefits. Standard errors in parentheses.

[b] Basic hourly wage. Hourly benefits in parentheses.

**Table B-7**
**New Orleans, Louisiana**

| Trade | Nonunion | | | Union[b] | | | Percent Union Wage Differential (Building) | Davis-Bacon[b] | |
|---|---|---|---|---|---|---|---|---|---|
| | Building | Residential | Heavy and Highway | Building | Residential | Heavy and Highway | | Commercial | Residential |
| **Bricklayer** | | | | | | | | | |
| Journeyman | 8.39 (.23) | 8.74 (.17) | — | 10.12 (.55) | 8.09 (.55) | | 21 | 10.12 (.585) | 6.00 |
| Helper | 4.88 (.27) | 4.22 (.07) | — | | | | | | |
| **Carpenter** | | | | | | | | | |
| Journeyman | 7.19 (.13) | 6.86 (.17) | 8.11 (.15) | 9.72 (.65) | — | | 35 | 9.72 (.69) | 5.00 |
| Helper | 5.17 (.32) | 3.55 (.06) | — | | | | | | |
| **Electrician** | | | | | | | | | |
| Journeyman | 6.20 (.06) | 7.14 (.35) | — | 10.60 (.71) | 6.15 (.36) | | 71 | 10.60 (.74) | 5.01 |
| Helper | 4.27 (.04) | — | — | | | | | | |
| **Ironworker** | | | | | | | | | |
| Journeyman | 6.59 (.07) | 5.79 (.02) | — | | | 10.17 total heavy | — | 9.86 (1.02) | 4.17 |
| Helper | 4.22 (.02) | — | — | | | | | | |
| **Operating Engineer** | | | | | | | | | |
| Journeyman | 6.18 (.09) | 5.75 (.16) | 8.11 (.37) | | | 9.43/0.73 heavy | — | 9.55 (.98) | 5.00 |
| Helper | — | | | | | | | | |

| | | | | | | | |
|---|---|---|---|---|---|---|---|
| Painter | | | | | | | |
| Journeyman | 4.75 (.23) | 4.85 (.20) | — | 7.78 (.58) | 64 | 7.775 (.625) | 4.50 |
| Helper | — | — | — | | | | |
| Plumbers and Pipefitters | | | | | | | |
| Journeyman | 7.28 | 5.47 (.22) | — | 10.30 (1.20) | 42 | 10.30 (1.28) | 5.50 |
| Helper | — | 3.72 (.09) | | | | | |
| Sheetmetal Workers | | | | | | | |
| Journeyman | 7.35 (.32) | 5.25 (.24) | | 9.81 (1.48) | 34 | 9.81 (1.58) | 4.55 |
| Helper | 3.67 (.12) | 3.61 (.07) | | | | | |
| Truck Driver | | | | | | | |
| Journeyman | — | 3.83 (.36) | | | | 4.10 | 3.50 |
| Helper | — | — | | | | | |
| Laborer | | | | | | | |
| Journeyman | 4.99 (.08) | 6.14 (.14) | | 7.27 (.20) | 46 | 7.07 (.40) | 3.04 |
| Helper | — | — | | | | | |

Mean Differential: 45%
Range: 21% to 71%

Source: 1976 Survey by the Department of Housing and Urban Development and the Massachusetts Institute of Technology.
[a]Hourly wage only, excluding benefits. Standard errors in parentheses.
[b]Basic hourly wage. Hourly benefits in parentheses.

**Table B-8**
**Portland, Oregon**

| Trade | Nonunion[a] | | | Union[b] | | | Percent Union Wage Differential (Building) | Davis-Bacon[b] | |
|---|---|---|---|---|---|---|---|---|---|
| | Building | Residential | Heavy and Highway | Building | Residential | Heavy and Highway | | Commercial | Residential |
| Bricklayer Journeyman | — (.42) | 7.94 | | 11.03 (1.40) | | | | 10.13 (1.38) | 9.42 (1.13) |
| Helper | — | — | | | | | | | |
| Carpenter Journeyman | 3.25 (.54) | 8.22 (.26) | | 10.09 (1.75) | 10.09 (1.75) | | 15 | 10.09 (1.68) | 7.29 (1.58) |
| Helper | 4.42 (.36) | 4.96 (.13) | | | | | | | |
| Electrician Journeyman | 9.73 (.44) | 8.89 (.22) | | 11.35 (1.46) | | | 17 | 11.35 (1.40) | 10.10 (.87) |
| Helper | — | 6.15 (.50) | | | | | | | |
| Ironworker Journeyman | — | — | | | | | — | 9.90 (1.88) | |
| Helper | — | — | | | | | | | |
| Operating Engineer Journeyman | 7.39 (.24) | 5.96 (.18) | 9.70 (.22) | 9.85 (2.50) | | | 33 | 9.85 (2.55) | 8.56 (1.80) (loader 4-6 cu.yds.) |
| Helper | 7.20 (.29) | — | | | | | | | |

| | Col 1 | Col 2 | Col 3 | Col 4 | Col 5 | Col 6 |
|---|---|---|---|---|---|---|
| **Painter** | | | | | | |
| Journeyman | — | 7.15 (.50) | — | — | 8.59 (1.13) | 7.77 (1.13) |
| Helper | — | — | — | | | |
| **Plumbers and Pipefitters** | | | | | | |
| Journeyman | 8.58 (1.77) | 6.17 (.17) | 12.00 (2.67) | 40 | 12.00 (2.80) | 9.37 (1.78) |
| Helper | 5.42 (1.20) | 5.39 (.89) | — | | | |
| **Roofer** | | | | | | |
| Journeyman | — | 7.40 (.30) | 9.95 (1.25) | — | 9.85 (1.20) | 9.05 (1.20) |
| Helper | — | — | — | | | |
| **Sheetmetal Worker** | | | | | | |
| Journeyman | 7.50 (.18) | 7.03 (.24) | 10.41 (2.68) | 39 | 8.71 (2.05) | 8.27 (1.50) |
| Helper | — | 6.25 (.82) | — | | | |
| **Truck Driver** | | | | | | |
| Journeyman | 7.55 (.18) | 6.92 (.21) | 9.53 (1.88) | 26 | 9.23 (1.93) | none |
| Helper | — | — | 9.00 (.12) | | | |
| **Laborer** | | | | | | |
| Journeyman | 5.98 | 6.44 | 8.55 (1.50) | 43 | 8.02 (2.40) | 6.55 (1.57) |
| Helper | — | — | 8.11 | | | |

Mean Differential: 30%
Range: 15% to 43%

Source: 1976 survey by the Department of Housing and Urban Development and the Massachusetts Institute of Technology.
aHourly wage only, excluding benefits. Standard errors in parentheses.
bBasic hourly wage. Hourly benefits in parentheses.

# Appendix C
# Contractor Interview
# Schedule

The following blank interview schedule shows the range of questions asked of contractors. Note that the one form was designed to be used with both union and open-shop firms. Questions in the center apply to all firms; those on the left apply to open-shop firms only; questions on the right apply to union firms only.

**A. Firm Type, Size, Employment Policy, History**

1. Are you primarily general_____or subcontractor_____or both_____?
2. What percentage of your work comes under the following categories?

   a. Residential (single family, townhouse, duplexes, all others less than 3 floors)_____%
   b. Residential (4 floors or more)_____%
   c. Commercial (stores, offices, warehouses, etc., less than 2 floors)_____%
   d. Commercial (3 floors or more)_____%
   e. Industrial (factories, power plants, etc.)_____%
   f. Institutional (schools, hospitals, etc.)_____%
   g. Highways (streets, roads, interstates)_____%
   h. Heavy (bridges, dams, sewers, etc.)_____%
   i. Other_____ _____%
   (specify)

3. What percentage of your work is public (either federal, state or local)?_____%
4. How many legal entities do you have (corporations, partnerships, etc.)?
   _____
5. What is your current monthly overhead? $_____
6. What is the current number of administrative people in your office?
   No._____
7. Do you have field people engaged exclusively as supervisors?_____
8. What year did the firm begin operation?_____
   year

Has the firm in the past ever operated as a "union" firm?
Yes___ No___ Occasionally___ (i.e., has signed
                   project agreements)
If "yes" or "occasionally", when was the last time? _____
                                       date

What was the main motivation for starting as or changing to a nonunion operation?

If now operating double-breasted, what is the main reason for this? (experimental; transitional; permanent: Why?)

Does this firm work with union contractors, either general or sub?
If "yes", what subs or trades? _____
(Have there been any major changes in work subcontracted in last 5 years?) _____
    If so, why?

Has the firm been subject to union organizing attempts or violence?

Has the firm in the past ever operated as a "nonunion" firm?
Yes___ No___ Occasionally___ (i.e., has signed
                   project agreements)
If "yes" or "occasionally", when was the last time? _____
                                         date

What was the main motivation for starting as or changing to a union operation?

Does this firm work with nonunion contractors, either general or sub?
If "yes", what subs or trades? _____
(Have there been any major changes in work subcontracted in last 5 years?) _____
    If so, why?

## B. Employment and Occupations

How many field employees do you keep on your payroll year-round? _____

How many *temporary* employees were employed on:
February 1, 1976 _____    July 1, 1976 _____

What percentage of these temporary employees are:

| | |
|---|---|
| Unskilled | (i.e., laborers) _____% |
| Semiskilled | (i.e., helpers) _____% |
| Skilled | (i.e., journeymen) _____% |

What trades or journeymen are typically on the firm's payroll?

Check: _____ Carpenters          _____ Plumbers
       _____ Laborers            _____ Electricians
       _____ Equipment Oper.
       _____ Other (specify): _____

In Your Experience, Do Union Journeymen Work Across Jurisdiction Lines for any Specific Reason or Purpose?

_____ Never

_____ Rarely, (If Work Demands It and Business Agent Permits It, etc.) Explain: _____

_____ Occasionally or Often. Explain: _____

In a Week, How Much Time Do These Journeymen Spend Performing Work Outside Their Crafts?

_____ Often    _____ Occasionally    _____ Rarely    _____ Never

If "Often" or "Occasionally", Which Journeymen or Crafts and What Else Do They Do?

| Primary Craft | Other Work |
|---|---|
| _____ | _____ |
| _____ | _____ |

Under What Conditions Do Journeymen Do Other Work?
   (Check one or more)

[ ] Tasks Related to Their Main Job—example: electrician doing some carpentry; plumbers digging trenches while laying pipe, etc.

[ ] Overlapping Work on Same Project—example: work crews on cement foundations; work crews on steel building erection.

[ ] During Seasonal Lows—example: stock or maintenance work.

[ ] Other: _____

Does Lack of Rigid Trade Jurisdictional Boundaries and/or Flexibility in Job Assignment Make It Easier to Maintain a Constant Work Force Year-round?

Yes _____    Somewhat _____    No _____

Since There Are No Jurisdictional Rules in Nonunion Construction, Are Your Journeymen Still Classified Along Trade or Craft Lines?

_____ Yes. Why? [ ] Nature of Construction Work
                [ ] Union Influence
                [ ] Davis-Bacon Reporting Requirement
_____ No.     [ ] Firm Doesn't Use Common Craft Classifications
                [ ] Other _____

Do You Use Other Noncraft Classifications for the Kind of Work Your Journeymen Do?

     Example: "Concrete Mechanic"; "Bridgemen"
     Other: _____

Does Firm Employ Semiskilled Workers (i.e., helpers, etc.)
If Not, Why Not?

Do These Helpers Work with Only One Trade or Do They Float Between Many Trades?

     Usually One Trade: (Example) _____
     Usually With Different Trades (Example) _____

Is There a Major Difference That Distinguishes a "Helper" from a Laborer or a Journeyman?

[ ] Yes, Helpers Have Some Knowledge or Specific Trades, Less Than Journeymen.

[ ] Yes, Helpers Have General Knowledge of Construction, More Than Laborers.

[ ] No, Some "Helpers" Are Just Laborers, Other Are Generally Skilled, Some Have a Few Specific Skills.

**C. Work Practices**

To Your Knowledge or Experience, Do Your Workers Use Any Tools or Equipment Which Union Journeymen Will Not Use?

Yes _____ No _____ Example: _____

To Your Knowledge, Do You Use Any Building Materials or Systems Not Permitted by Union Contracts?

Yes _____ No _____ Example: _____

Does the Firm Have Specific Work Rules on Use of Equipment—Other Than "Best Practice" or "Safety Rules"?

Yes _____ No _____ Example: _____

**C. Work Practices**

In Your Experience, Do Your Union Journeymen Refuse to Use Any Tool or Equipment on the Job Which You Would Prefer to Use?

_____ Yes, restrictions exist but are not enforced.
_____ Yes, restrictions exist and are enforced.
_____ Yes, restrictions did exist at one time.

Example: _____

_____ No

In Your Experience, Do Union Journeymen Refuse to Use Any Particular Building Materials or Systems (or Affect Use or Them)?

_____ Yes, now refuse to
_____ Yes, used to refuse to
How or why changed? _____
_____ No

Are There Any Work Rules on Use of Equipment or Work Methods That Are in Present Union Contracts and Enforced?

_____ Yes, example:
_____ No, but existed in past example:
How or why changed? _____
_____ No

**D. Wages and Productivity**

In the Trades You Hire, Do You Think There Should Be a "Helper" or Any Other Form of "Lesser Skilled" Worker (with Commensurately Lower Pay)?

Yes _____ Example: _____
No _____

Specify Ratio of Journeymen to Apprentices (and Helpers, if Any) Permitted by Union Contract. _____

Are Your Journeymen Equally Productive? _____

**D. Wages and Productivity**

What Explains the Wage Variations, if any, Your Firm Pays to Different Laborers, Helpers or Journeymen?

[ ] No Variations. Why?

Comment: _____

Variations Due To:

[ ] Experience
[ ] Mechanical Skill
[ ] Aptitude
[ ] Supervisory Capability
[ ] Loyalty
[ ] Length of Employment
[ ] Attitude
[ ] Other _____ (specify)

Do You Usually:

[ ] Bargain Wage Increases Individually with Each Employee
[ ] Grant Across-the-Board Increases
[ ] Combination of Individual and Across-the-Board Wage Increases

Specify Ratio of Journeymen (or Craftsmen) to Helpers on Typical Job. _____

Do You Pay Workers Extra for Travel Costs or Travel Time?
Always_____ Occasionally_____ Never_____

Do You Pay Extra for Hazardous Work—Such as Underground or on Heights?
Always_____ Occasionally_____ Never_____

If You Do "Scale" Work, Do You:

[ ] Rotate Men Through This Work—To Give All Equal Share of High-Wage Work
[ ] Separate Crews
[ ] Other _____ (specify)

Do These Scale Rates Influence Wages on *Private* Construction?

[ ] Yes: Firm Pays Scale on All Work
[ ] Some: Firm Pays Higher Than Average Due to Scale
[ ] No

Which of the Following Factors Do You Think *Most* Contribute to the Productivity of Your Work Force?

[ ] Workers Skill and Initiative Rewarded Individually
[ ] Workers Not Interested in Restricting Output
[ ] Ability to Fire Unproductive Workers
[ ] Workers Have Commitment to Company
[ ] Contractor's Right to Manage On-site Work
[ ] Other _____ (specify)

What Factor Most Contributes to the Differences in the Productivity?

[ ] Workers' Skill and Initiative Rewarded Individually
[ ] Workers Not Interested in Restricting Output
[ ] Ability to Fire Unproductive Workers
[ ] Workers Have Commitment to Company
[ ] Contractor's Right to Manage On-site Work
[ ] Other _____ (Specify)

Do You Hire Former Nonunion Journeymen, Apprentices, or Workers With Nonunion Experience?
Often_____ Occasionally_____ Never_____
Specify Trade: _____

What Sources Do You Normally Use for Hiring Field Workers?

Newspaper want ads
State employment service
At gate of project site
At main office
Other: Example: _____

Comment: _____

Is There a Central Labor Referral System Other Than Those Sponsored by Federal, State, or Local Authorities?

Yes _____ No _____

(a) If Yes, Does It Serve Your Needs?

Yes _____
No _____ Why Not? _____

(b) If No, Is Any Type of Central Labor Exchange or Referral System Needed?

Yes _____
No _____ Why Not? _____

Do You Hire Former Union Journeymen, Apprentices, or Workers?

Often _____ Occasionally _____ Never _____

Specify Trade: _____

When You Faced Any Year-round Scarcity of Skills or Manpower, When Was It and In What Trade(s)?

In a Peak Period, What Sources Do You Use to Recruit Workers?

[ ] Recruit From Other Areas
[ ] Recruit From Other Contractors
[ ] Upgrade and Train Less Skilled Men
[ ] Other _____
                    (specify)

Are These Source Adequate? Comment:

## E. Training

Do You Employ Apprentices?

No_____

Yes_____ In Which Trades?_____
_____

(a) If Yes, Are These Apprentices Enrolled in Certified Training Programs?

Yes_____ No_____

Do You Feel That Formal Apprentice Programs Are Necessary to Train Your Workers?

[ ] Yes, For All Trades

[ ] Yes, But Only for Some Trades (specify)_____

_____ and Not For_____
_____

[ ] No

If "No", What Are the Reasons?

[ ] Too Long

[ ] Too Complicated For Most Workers

[ ] Too Expensive

[ ] Other_____

(specify)

Do You Use Any Nonapprentice Training Programs?

Yes_____ No_____

If "Yes", What Kind?

[ ] On-the-Job Training

[ ] Informal Training After Hours

[ ] Special Short Courses

[ ] Other_____

(specify)

Roughly, To What Extent Are Your Foremen and Supervisor Apprentice Trained?

Estimate_____ %

# Bibliography

Abrams, Philip. Statement for the Associated Builders and Contractors, Inc. before the Subcommittee on Housing and Urban Affairs of the Senate Committee on Banking, Housing, and Urban Affairs, May 2, 1979.

AFL-CIO Building Trades Department. *The Davis-Bacon Act: It Works to Build America*. Washington, D.C., 1979.

Allen, Steven. "Unionized Construction Workers are More Productive." Unpublished, North Carolina State University, 1979.

Ashenfelter, Orley. "Union Relative Wage Effects: New Evidence and a Survey of Their Implications for Wage Inflation." Mimeographed. Princeton, N.J.: Princeton University, May 1976.

Ashenfelter, Orley and Johnson, George. "Unionism, Relative Wages, and Labor Quality in U.S. Manufacturing Industry." *International Economic Review*, October 1972.

Barbarsh, Jack. "Union Interests in Apprenticeship and Other Training Forms." *Journal of Human Resources* 3 (1968).

Blaney, James. "A Comparison of Occupational Structure in Union and Nonunion Residential Construction." S.M. thesis, Department of Civil Engineering, Massachusetts Institute of Technology, 1977.

Borcherching, John. "Improving Productivity in Industrial Construction by Effective Management of Human Resources." *Project Management Institute Proceedings*, Montreal: 1976.

Bourdon, Clinton C. "Pattern Bargaining, Wage Determination, and Inflation," in *Unemployment and Inflation: Institutionalist and Structuralist Views*, M.J. Piore ed.. M.E. Sharpe, 1979.

Bourdon, Clinton C., and Levitt, Raymond E. "A Comparison of Wages and Labor Management Practices in Union and Nonunion Construction." Department of Civil Engineering, Massachusetts Institute of Technology, 1978.

Brown, Charles and Medoff, James. "Trade Unions in the Production Process." *Journal of Political Economy* 86, no. 3 (1978):355-378.

Burke, Gilbert. "A Time of Reckoning for the Building Unions." *Fortune*, June 4, 1979.

Business Roundtable. *Coming to Grips With Some Major Problems in the Construction Industry*. Business Roundtable Report 2 (New York, 1978):25.

Cababa, Robin R. "An Analysis of Non-Apprentice Forms of Training in Construction." S.M. thesis, Department of Civil Engineering, Massachusetts Institute of Technology, 1976.

Center to Protect Workers' Rights. *The GAO on Davis-Bacon: A Fatally Flawed Study*, Washington, D.C., September 1979.

Chamber of Commerce of the United States. "National Conference on Construction Problems." Task Force Report, July 1969.

Chamberlain, Neil. *The Union Challenge to Management Control*. New York: Harper and Row, 1948.

Clark, Kim. "Unionization, Management Adjustment, and Productivity." National Bureau of Economic Research, Working Paper No. 332, Cambridge, Mass., April 1979.

Colean, Miles L. and Newcomb, Robinson. *Stabilizing Construction: The Record and Potential*. New York: McGraw-Hill, 1952.

Collins, W. and Logcher, Robert D. "The Effects of Management on Construction Labor Productivity." American Society of Civil Engineers *Journal of Construction Division*, Vol. 104 CO2, June, 1978.

Construction Labor Report, No. 1008, Sept. 1, 1976, p. A-19.

Construction Labor Report, No. 1129, June 22, 1977, p. A-13.

Contractors Mutual Association. "Trends in Open Shop Construction." December, 1975.

Council on Wage and Price Stability. "An Analysis of Certain Aspects of the Administration of the Davis-Bacon Act." Washington, D.C., June 25, 1976.

Cullen, Donald E. and Feinberg, Louis. *The Bargaining Structure in Construction: Problems and Prospects*, Unpublished, January 1979.

Diehl, Donald and Penner, Wayman. *Commercial Carpentry*. Washington, D.C. and Stillwater, Okla.: Associated General Contractors and Oklahoma State Department of Vocational and Technical Education, 1974.

Donahue, Charles. "The Davis-Bacon Act and the Walsh-Healy Act: A Comparison of Coverage and Minimum Wage Provisions." *Law and Contemporary Problems*.

Dunlop, John T. "The Industrial Relations System in Construction." In *The Structure of Collective Bargaining*, edited by Arnold Weber. New York: Free Press, 1961.

Flanagan, Robert. "Wage Interdependence in Unionized Labor Markets." *Brookings Papers in Economic Activity*, 1976:2.

Foster, Howard G. *Manpower in Homebuilding: A Preliminary Analysis*. Philadelphia: University of Pennsylvania Press, 1974.

Franklin, William S. "Are Construction Apprenticeships Too Long?" *Labor Law Journal*, February 1976, pp. 99-106.

Freeman, Richard and Medoff, James. "What Do Unions Do?" Harvard Institute of Economic Research. Working Paper No. 586, Cambridge, Mass., November 1977.

Georgine, Robert A., Testimony before the Subcommittee on Housing and Urban Affairs of the Senate Committee on Banking, Housing, and Urban Affairs, May 2, 1979.

Gibbons, Michael W. "The Declining Role of Craft Unions in the Construction Industry." B.A. honors thesis in economics, Harvard College, March 23, 1978. (Portions reprinted in this book with permission of the author.)

Gould, John P., *Davis-Bacon Act: The Economics of Prevailing Wage Laws* (America Enterprise Institute, Washington, D.C., 1971).

Goldfarb, Robert S. and Morral, John F., III. "Cost Implications of Changing Davis-Bacon Administration." Mimeographed. Washington, D.C., May 1975.

Gujarati, D.N., "The Economics of the Davis-Bacon Act." *Journal of Business*, July 1967, pp. 303-316.

Haber, William. *Industrial Relations in the Building Industry.* 2d ed. New York: Arno Press, 1971.

Haber, William and Levinson, Harold M. *Labor Relations and Productivity in the Building Trades.* Ann Arbor: University of Michigan Press, 1956.

Hall, Robert E. "The Role of Prevailing Prices and Wages in the Efficient Organization of Markets." National Bureau of Economic Research, Working Paper No. 386, August 1979.

Hintze, Arthur. "Taking the Waste Out of Davis-Bacon." *Constructor*, June 1977.

Johnson, George E. "Economic Analysis of Trade Unionism." *Papers and Proceedings of the American Economic Association*, May 1975, pp. 23-28.

Kerr, Clark. "The Balkanization of Labor Markets." In *Labor Mobility and Economic Opportunity*, edited by E.W. Bakke et al., Cambridge: MIT Press, 1954.

Lewis, H. Gregg. *Unionism and Relative Wages in the U.S.* Chicago: University of Chicago Press, 1963.

Lipsky, David B. and Farber, Henry S. "The Composition of Strike Activity in the Construction Industry." *Industrial and Labor Relations Review* 29 (1976):388-404.

Machnik, Nicholas Jan. "Subcontracting in the U.S. Construction Industry." S.M. thesis, Department of Civil Engineering, Massachusetts Institute of Technology, 1977.

Mandelstamm, Allan B. "The Effects of Unions on Efficiency in the Residential Construction Industry: A Case Study." *Industrial and Labor Relations Review* 18 (1965):503-521.

Marshall, Ray; Glover, Robert W.; and Franklin, William S. *Training and Entry Into Union Construction.* U.S. Department of Labor Manpower Administration Monograph 39, U.S. Government Printing Office, 1975.

Mattila, John and Mattila, Peter. "Construction Apprenticeship in the Detroit Labor Market." *Industrial Relations*, February 1976.

Mills, D.Q. "Wage Determination in Contract Construction." *Industrial Relations*, February 1971.

Mills, D.Q. "Collective Bargaining in Construction," in G. Somers, ed., *Contemporary Collective Bargaining*. Industrial Relations Research Association, Madison, Wisc., 1977.

Mills, Daniel Quinn. "The Labor Force and Industrial Relations." In Contractor's Management Handbook, edited by J. O'Brien and R. Zilly. Englewood Cliffs, N.J.: McGraw-Hill, 1971.

Mills, D. Quinn. *Industrial Relations and Manpower in Construction*. Cambridge: MIT Press, 1972.

*National Industrial Construction Agreement*. National Constructors Association and several international building trades unions. 1978.

Northrup, Herbert R. and Foster, Howard G. *Open Shop Construction*. Philadelphia: University of Pennsylvania Press, 1975.

O'Brien, James J. and Zilly, Robert G., *Contractor's Management Handbook*. Englewood Cliffs, N.J.: McGraw-Hill, 1971.

Olsen, John G. "Labor and Material Requirements for New School Construction." *Monthly Labor Review*, April 1979.

Oaxaca, R.L. "Estimation of Union/Nonunion Wage Differentials Within Occupational Regional Subgroups." *Journal of Human Resources*, Fall 1975, pp. 529-536.

Ouichi, William G. "The Relation Between Organizational Structure and Organizational Control." *Administrative Sciences Quarterly*, March 1977, pp. 95-113.

Parnes, H.S. et al. *The National Longitudinal Survey of Older Men*. University of Michigan, 1971.

Rees, Albert. *The Economics of Trade Unions*. Chicago: University of Chicago Press, 1962.

Reinecke, Royce M. "Quantitative Methods for Measuring the Size of the Nonunion Sector of the Construction Industry." S.M. thesis, Department of Civil Engineering, Massachusetts Institute of Technology, 1977.

Rosefielde, Steven and Mills, D.Q. "Is the Construction Industry Technologically Stagnant?" in *The Construction Industry*, edited by D.Q. Mills and Julian Lange. Lexington, Mass.: D.C. Heath and Co., Lexington Books, 1979.

Rossow, Janet. "The Role of Technology in the Productivity of Highway Construction in the U.S." Ph.D. dissertation, Department of Civil Engineering, Massachusetts Institute of Technology, February 1977.

Rossow, Janet and Moavenzadeh, Fred. "Productivity and Technology Change in Construction." American Society of Civil Engineers Preprint No. 3597, ASCE Convention, Boston, April 2-6, 1979.

Segal, Martin. "Union Wage Impact and Market Structure." *Quarterly Journal of Economics*, February 1964.

Smith, Arthur, Jr. "Boycotts of Prefabricated Building Products and the Regulation of Technological Change in Construction Jobsites." *Industrial and Labor Relations Review*, January 1972.

Solomon, Arthur and Bourdon, Clinton C. "The Inflationary Effects of the Davis-Bacon Act: A Critique of the Research Literature." Unpublished, Cambridge, Mass., July 1979.

Speed, William S. "Construction Labor Cost Comparison of Open and Closed Shop Construction Projects." *Proceedings of the Annual Convention of the American Association of Cost Engineers*, 1978.

Stinchcombe, A.L. "Bureaucratic and Craft Administration of Production." *Administrative Sciences Quarterly*, 1960, pp. 168-187.

Strand, Kenneth. *Jurisdictional Disputes in Construction*. Pullman: Washington State University Press, 1961.

Thieblot, Armand. *The Davis-Bacon Act*. University of Pennsylvania Press, 1975.

U.S. Bureau of the Census. *Census of Construction Industries: 1972*. Washington, D.C.: U.S. Government Printing Office, 1976.

U.S. Bureau of Labor Statistics. *Industrial Wage Survey: Contract Construction*, Bulletin 1911. Washington, D.C.: U.S. Government Printing Office, 1976.

U.S. Department of Labor, Labor Management Services Administration. *Exclusive Work Referral Systems in the Building Trades*. Washington, D.C.: U.S. Government Printing Office, 1970.

U.S. Department of Labor. "Wage Rate Determination Procedures." *Federal Register*, vol. 37, no. 194, October 5, 1972.

U.S. Department of Labor, Bureau of Labor Statistics. *Job Seeking Methods Used by Americans as Workers*, Bulletin 1886. Washington, D.C.: U.S. Government Printing Office, 1975.

U.S. General Accounting Office. *The Davis-Bacon Act Should Be Repealed*. Washington, D.C., April 27, 1979.

Vander Els, David. "An Analysis of Apprenticeship Training in the Non-Union Sector of the Construction Industry." S.M. thesis, Department of Civil Engineering, Massachusetts Institute of Technology, 1976.

Weinstein, Paul. "Featherbedding: A Theoretical Analysis." In *Featherbedding and Technological Change*, edited by Paul Weinstein. Lexington, Mass., Lexington Books, D.C. Heath, 1965.

Williamson, Oliver E.; Wachter, M.L.; and Harris, J.E. "Understanding the Employment Relation: The Analysis of Idiosyncratic Exchange." *Bell Journal of Economics*, Spring 1975.

# Index

# Index

# About the Authors

**Clinton C. Bourdon** is an assistant professor of business administration at the Harvard Graduate School of Business Administration. He received the Ph.D. in economics and urban studies from the Massachusetts Institute of Technology after receiving degrees from Brown University and Harvard University. He has taught economics at Amherst College and Boston University and has worked on economic development problems in Chile, Mexico, Italy, and Libya. He has also been a consultant to the U.S. Departments of Labor, Commerce, and Housing and Urban Development; the Commonwealth of Massachusetts; the New York State Urban Development Corporation; and several construction firms. His current research focuses on productivity and technological change in manufacturing as well as in construction and on collective-bargaining strategies in several major industries.

**Raymond E. Levitt** is an associate professor of construction management in the Civil Engineering Department of the Massachusetts Institute of Technology. He received the bachelor's degree in civil engineering and the M.S. and Ph.D. degrees in construction management from Stanford University. His current teaching and research interests are in organization theory, management information systems, and labor relations in construction. He has been a consultant to contractors, designers, and users in all sectors of the construction industry, as well as to agencies of state and federal government. He is a member of the U.S. National Committee on Tunneling Technology and is trustee of the Project Management Institute's New England Chapter.